"Words From The Wise To Enlighten One's Mind"

BRANDON T. MITCHELL

ISBN-10: 1500482072
ISBN-13: 978-1500482077

BRANDON T. MITCHELL

CONTENTS

INTRODUCTION

Through the Lord (Jesus Christ), I have been blessed with legend-ability to create unique thoughts and share different perspectives to have others think of what they say before they speak.

Legend to me stands for:

A LEG to stand strong on what you believe to the END; Standing strong on what you know and being the best at your trade.

Take your memories into a legacy, so that other generations can have a **LEG** to stand strong – **A**nd – **CY**/See, from another perspective, so that you can shine on others.

> *I can do all things through Christ which strengtheneth me* *(Philippians 4:13).* *Let your light so shine before men, that they may see your good works, and glorify your Father which is in heaven (Matthew 5:16).*

When you allow your light to shine, you will become a manifestation of knowledge. That's a brighter light (as the sun) to the hearts and souls for others, by giving them a dose of laughter, for medicine, in which no earthly doctor can prescribe nor provide.

> *Then was our mouth filled with laughter, and our tongue with singing: then said they among the heathen, the Lord hath done great things for them. The Lord hath done great things for us; whereof we are glad (Psalms 126:2-3). A merry heart doeth good like a medicine: but a broken spirit drieth the bones (Proverbs 17:22).*

ACKNOWLEGEMENTS

This book is dedicated to my God. It is He who had given me the inspiration to write this book. It allows me and others who read this book to speak, think, and live a godly life style.

I would like to thank my fiancée (Tania Woods) for her assistance and time in helping me with this book.

Unless otherwise indicated, all Scripture quotations are from the Holy Bible, King James Version, copyright © 1990 by Thomas Nelson, Inc. and the New Spirit Filled Life Bible, New King James Version, copyright © 2002 By Thomas Nelson, Inc.

"WORDS FROM THE WISE TO ENLIGHTEN ONE'S MIND"

CHAPTER 1

FOOD FOR THOUGHT

As Christians, we are passing through, on earth, as visitors. But, when the Lord opens the gates of our new residence, we are there for eternity.

*For our light affliction, which is but for a moment, worketh for us a far more exceeding and eternal weight of glory **(II Corinthians 4:17)**; For we are strangers before thee, and sojourners, as were all our fathers: our days on the earth are as a shadow, and there is none abiding **(I Chronicles 29:15)**. Whereas ye know not what shall be on the morrow. For what is your life? It is even a vapour, that appeareth for a time, and then vanisheth away **(James 4:14)**.*

It is said that time doesn't last forever. But, that you are my time of joy, can you be my forever?

> *Blessed is he that readeth, and they that hear the words of this prophecy, and keep those things which are written therein: for the time is at hand* **(Revelations 1:3)**. *But rejoice, inasmuch as ye are partakers of Christ's sufferings; that, when his glory shall be revealed, ye may be glad also with exceeding joy* **(I Peter 4:13)**. *These things have I written unto you that believe on the name of the Son of God; that ye may know that ye have eternal life, and that ye may believe on the name of the Son of God* **(I John 5:13)**.

It's the Holy Spirit who thinks ahead through us, but the Lord also gives us a head to think.

> *But when they shall lead you, and deliver you up, take no thought beforehand what ye shall speak, never do ye premeditate: but whatsoever shall be given you in that hour, that speak ye: for it is not ye that speak, but the Holy Ghost* **(Mark 13:11)**. *Who hath put wisdom in the inward parts? or who hath given understanding to the heart* **(Job 38:36)**? *Let this mind be in you, which was also in Christ Jesus* **(Philippians 2:5)**.

God will always have for us a harvest, but it is us who makes reaping the hardest.

> *Then saith He unto His disciples,* *The harvest truly is plenteous, but the labourers are few; Pray ye therefore the Lord of the harvest, that He will send forth labourers into His harvest* **(Matthew 9:37-38)**.

We are told to bounce back, but if we do so, we attend to the past. Therefore, we should spring forward.

VS

Moreover, if we bounce back, Satan can have a ball on us. But, if we spring forward, we can rise to new heights.

> *Remember ye not the former things, neither consider the things of old* **(Isaiah 43:18-19)**. *Therefore if any man be in Christ, he is a new creature: old things are passed away; behold, all things are become new* **(II Corinthians 5:17)**.

Kids were playing in a restaurant as they were also trying to keep the baby under control. The baby banged her head under the table and started to cry. The adults got up from the table to put the baby's coat on. The baby said, very clearly, "Bye (as she suddenly stopped crying)! Sometimes, it takes the head of a baby to think for adults. *(True Story)*

*And I will give children to be their princes, and babes shall rule over them **(Isaiah 3:4)**.*

You have to speak peace to seek peace.

*What man is he that desireth life, and loveth many days, that he may see good? Keep thy tongue from evil, and thy lips from speaking guile. Depart from evil, and do good; seek peace, and pursue it **(Psalms 34:12-14)**.*

As a couple were walking out of a building, it was raining with the wind blowing hard. The guy's umbrella took a shift in an upward position. As rain was pouring down on him, he needed a shield of protection. Therefore, his wife walking beside him had an extra umbrella where they both shared.

God's plan for husband and wife is to operate under the same umbrella, and to never become separated, especially through the storms.

*Therefore shall a man leave his father and his mother, and shall cleave unto his wife: and they shall be one flesh **(Genesis 2:24)**. And the rain descended, and the floods came, and the winds blew, and beat upon that house; and it fell not: for it was founded upon a rock **(Matthew 7:25)**.*

One day, I looked around the house for my phone for about one hour, and I could not find it. Since I could not find my phone, I started saying to the Lord, "I wish phones can talk." One minute later, I heard my voicemail come on. I guess that rings a bell. I said, "Thank you Lord!" The word says, "Ask and you shall receive." On the voicemail, my little niece was playing with her mother's cell phone and said, "Calling for Brandon on planet earth." The Lord also speaks through the mouths of babes. *(True Story)*

> *If ye abide in me, and my words abide in you, ye shall ask what ye will, and it shall be done unto you* **(John 15:7)**. *And this is the confidence that we have in Him, that, if we ask any thing according to His will, He heareth us: And if we know that He hear us, whatsoever we ask, we know that we have the petitions that we desire of Him* **(I John 5:14-15)**. *At that time Jesus answered and said, I thank thee, O Father, Lord of heaven and earth, because thou hast hid these things from the wise and prudent, and hast revealed them unto babes* **(Matthew11:25)**. *In thee, O LORD, do I put my trust: let me never be put to confusion* **(Psalm 71:1)**.

A man that's in the word each day of the week can make him spiritually strong.

Staying spiritually strong in the word.

On the contrary a man that has a stronghold, and out of word each day, can make him spiritually weak.

Staying spiritually weak Out of the word.

Therefore I take pleasure in infirmities, in reproaches, in necessities, in persecutions, in distresses for Christ's sake: for when I am weak, then am I strong **(II Corinthians 12:10)**. *But his delight is in the law of the LORD; and in His law doth he mediate day and night* **(Psalms 1:2-3)**.

A Pastor called a young man, by the name of Dexter, up to the altar to pray for both his feet. The Bishop (by the Holy Spirit), told Dexter to sit down, take his shoes off, and for him to touch his own feet. The Bishop said, "Thank God!" Dexter started to thank God for his healing, and his feet were healed. Little did Dexter know, the Bishop was thanking God, because he did not have to touch his feet. Many times, words that people speak are meant for bad, but God can turn them around to mean something good.

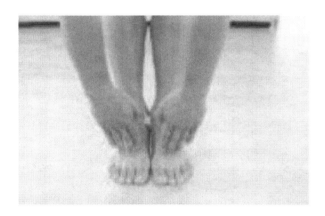

But as for you, ye thought evil against me; but God meant it unto good, to bring to pass, as it is this day, to save much people alive ***(Genesis 50:20)***. *And we know that all things work together for good to them that love God, to them who are the called according to His purpose* ***(Romans 8:28)***.

If you continue to rehearse the situation, you will bruise the wound. In order for God to heal your pains, you have to give Him room.

*Who hath woe? who hath sorrow? who hath contentions? who hath babbling? who hath wounds without cause? who hath redness of eyes **(Proverbs 23:29)**? Forbearing one another, if any man have a quarrel against any: even as Christ forgave us, so also do ye **(Colossians 3:13)**. Jesus answered, I have told you that I am He: if therefore ye seek me, let these go there way **(John 18:8)**: And God shall wipe away all tears from their eyes; and there shall be no more death, neither sorrow, nor crying, neither shall there be any more pain: for the former things are passed away **(Revelation 21:4)**. As many as I love, I rebuke and chasten: be zealous therefore, and repent. Behold, I stand at the door, and knock: if any man hear my voice, and open the door, I will come in to him, and will sup with him, and he with Me. To him that overcometh will I grant to sit with Me in my throne, even as I also overcame, and am set down with My Father in His throne **(Revelations 3:19-21)**.*

It's something how we race people to reach to our destinations. We cut in front of each other; we talk and cut someone else off; we rush to try and beat others taking a test; we cut people off in traffic during rush hour; and many of us take so many credit hours per semester (in college), that we rush to graduate. There are many other examples of racing to our destinations. The Lord gives us life with a race of our own. Why can't we live with that, and let God handle our battles.

I returned, and saw under the sun, that the race is not to the swift, nor the battle to the strong, neither yet bread to the wise, nor yet riches to men of understanding, nor yet favour to men of skill; but time and chance happeneth to them all **(Ecclesiastes 9:11)**. *And He said, Hearken ye, all Judah, and ye inhabitants of Jerusalem, and thou king Je-hosh'-a-phat, Thus saith the Lord unto you, Be not afraid nor dismayed by reason of this great multitude; for the battle is not your's but God's* **(II Chronicles 20:15)**.

At moments, there is all work and no play, but it's the jerk who tries to get in our way. The jerk is Satan, who's always waiting to detain our minds to try and keep us blind. But, the Lord will come to your rescue. It is He who has the best for you.

Knowing that a man is not justified by the works of the law, but by the faith of Jesus Christ, even we have believed in Jesus Christ, that we might be justified be the faith of Christ, and not by the works of the law: for by the works of the law shall no flesh be justified **(Galatians 2:16)**. *Put them in mind to be subject to principalities and powers, to obey magistrates, to be ready to every good work, to speak evil of no man, to be no brawlers, but gentle, shewing all meekness unto all men. For we ourselves also were sometimes foolish, disobedient, deceived, serving divers lusts and pleasures, living in malice and envy, hateful, and hating one another. But after the kindness and love of God our Saviour toward man appeared, not by works of righteousness which we have done, but according to His mercy He saved us, by the washing of regeneration, and renewing of the Holy Ghost; which He shed on us abundantly Saviour; that being justified by His grace, we should be made heirs according to the hope of eternal life* **(Titus 3:1-7)**. *And call upon Me in the day of trouble: I will deliver thee, and thou shalt glorify Me* **(Psalm 50:15)**.

Why is "Forgive" called "Forgive"?

Because: For. = the abbreviation of Forward
Give = love.

For one to forgive another, is to look and move forward from the past, by giving or expressing love.

The keywords are *forward* and *give*. When you separate the word *forward,* you get *for* and *ward.* You also have the word *give*. Therefore, when you *for/give*, you will reap your *re/ward*.

> *Judge not, and ye shall not be judged: condemn not, and ye shall not be condemned: forgive, and ye shall be forgiven **(Luke 6:37)**: For if ye forgive men their trespasses, your heavenly Father will also forgive you: But if ye forgive not men their trespasses, neither will your Father forgive your trespasses **(Matthew 6:14-15)**.*

Our errors in life are not from our chancing it, but it's meant for our enhancement.

> *A wise man will hear, and will increase learning; and a man of understanding shall attain unto wise counsels **(Proverbs 1:5)**: Give instruction to a wise man, and he will be yet wiser: teach a just man, and he will increase in learning **(Proverbs 9:9)**.*

If you have no room for change, then you will have no room for God. If you don't have room for God, then you will mess up, because God is up. To elaborate, God don't like mess, and "Up" is positive. Everything about God is positive. Therefore, don't mess "Up".

No man can serve two masters: for either he will Hate the one, and love the other; or else he will hold to the one, and despise the other. Ye cannot serve God and mammon **(Matthew 6:24)**. *But now, after that ye have known God, or rather are known of God, how turn ye again to the weak and beggarly elements, whereunto ye desire again to be in bondage* **(Galatians 4:9)**?

Be patient with the Lord, because if it's in His will, your desires will be assured.

And we desire that every one of you do shew the same diligence to the full assurance of hope unto the end: That ye be not slothful, but followers of them who through faith and patience inherit the promises. For when God made promise to Abraham, because he could swear by no greater, he sware by himself, saying, SURELY BLESSING I WILL BLESS THEE, AND MULTIPLYING I WILL MULTIPLY TREE. And so, after he had patiently endured, he obtained the promise **(Hebrews 6:11-15)**. *Delight thyself also in the LORD; and He shall give thee the desires of thine heart* **(Psalm 37:4)**.

When you take positive chances in life, it's to give you advances in life. If you don't try the unknown, you will stay in one zone.

Therefore we conclude that a man is justified by faith without the deeds of the law **(Romans 3:28)**.

Put God first and He will nurse your thirst. He will do it to completion and fight your battles to deletion. He will do it day by day, when you have faith in Him, and when you pray.

But seek ye first the kingdom of God, and His righteousness; and all these things shall be added unto you **(Matthew 6:33)**.

It's the Holy Spirit who thinks ahead through us, but the Lord also gives us a head to think.

But when they shall lead you, and deliver you up, take no thought beforehand what ye shall speak, never do ye premeditate: but whatsoever shall be given you in that hour, that speak ye: for it is not ye that speak, but the Holy Ghost **(Mark 13:11)**. *Who hath put wisdom in the inward parts? or who hath given understanding to the heart* **(Job 38:36)**? *Let this mind be in you, which was also in Christ Jesus* **(Philippians 2:5)**.

Many people seem to show no fear by living in the hood, where a bullet can go through so easily. Why is it that we are so slow to abide in God's word who is our shield of protection from all darts?

He shall cover thee with his feathers, and under wings shalt thou trust: his truth shall be thy shield and buckler. Thou shalt not be afraid for the terror by night; nor for the arrow that fileth by day **(Psalms 91:4-5)**; *Above all, taking the shield of faith, wherewith ye shall be able to quench all the fiery darts of the wicked. And take the helmet of salvation, and the sword of the Spirit, which is the word of God* **(Ephesians 6:16-17)**.

I had a talk with a woman by the name of Diamond, who said that she didn't know what her gift was nor her purpose in life. Diamond stated that she was chicken to do ministry. I replied, "You should never claim yourself to be chicken. That only allows Satan to eat you up."

*Be not deceived; God is not mocked: for whatsoever a man soweth, that shall he also reap (**Galatians 6:7**). A man's gift maketh room for him, and bringeth him before great men (**Proverbs 18:16**). For God hath not given us the spirit of fear; but of power, and of love, and of a sound mind (**II Timothy1:7**). And there are three that bear witness in earth, the spirit, and the water, and the blood: and these three agree in one (**II Peter 5:8**).*

If you don't live by the Holy Ghost, in the fire you may roast.

> *Verily I say unto you, All sins shall be forgiven unto the sons of men, and blasphemies wherewith soever they shall blaspheme: But he that shall blaspheme against the Holy Ghost hath never forgiveness, but is in danger of eternal damnation* **(Mark 3:28-29)**: *The steps of a good man are ordered by the LORD: and he delighteth in his way. Though he fall, he shall not be utterly cast down: for the LORD upholdeth him with His hand* **(Psalms 37:23-24)**.

The things to look forward to, you are blinded by them, because the things of the past, in looking back, you are reminded of them. Moreover, if you are looking back, how can you see in front of you?

> *FOR YET A LITTLE WHILE, AND HE THAT SHALL COME WILL COME, AND WILL NOT TARRY. NOW THE JUST SHALL LIVE BY FAITH: BUT IF ANY MAN DRAW BACK, MY SOUL SHALL HAVE NO PLEASURE IN HIM. But we are not of them who draw back unto perdition; but of them that believe to the saving of the soul* **(Hebrews 10:37-39)**. *And Jesus said unto him,* No man, having put his hand to the plough, and looking back, is fit for the kingdom of God **(Luke 9:62)**.

When you snap at people, Satan uses it as a tune to dance as a snapping of fingers to a melody.

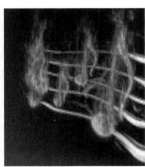

*BE YE ANGRY, AND SIN NOT: let not the sun go down on your wrath **(Ephesians 4:26-27)**: A SOFT answer turneth away wrath: but grievous words stir up anger. The tongue of the wise useth knowledge aright: but the mouth of fools poureth out foolishness **(Proverbs 15:1-2)**.*

God is our Alpha and Omega. Why is God, also after us? Because the Lord is our protection around us. Furthermore, if the Lord isn't after us, then Satan would be after us. God has to be after us to keep Satan off of us. Moreover, God has to be our Alpha and Omega to be a shield around us for our protection.

*I am Alpha and Omega, the beginning and the ending, saith the Lord, which is, and which was, and which is to come, the Almighty **(Revelation 1:8)**.*

The Lord's word taste divine at all times. You can have it as a treat and it taste so sweet. You can eat it everyday, with 0 calories, so you won't gain weight.

*O taste and see that the LORD is good: blessed is the man that trusteth in Him **(Psalm 34:8)**.*

A lady and a man was waiting on a bus. When the lady saw the numbers on both buses, she said, "That's not our bus." I told the lady, "Anything can be yours, you just have to claim it."

*And Jesus answering saith unto them, Have faith in God. For verily I say unto you, That whosoever shall say into this mountain, Be thou removed, and be thou cast into the sea; and shall not doubt in his heart, but shall believe that those things which he saith shall come to pass; he shall have whatsoever he saith **(Mark 11:22-23)**.*

A man once said, "I am never lost for words." Many people can be lost for words. It depends on who's giving directions.

*Trust in the LORD with all thine heart; and lean not unto thine own understanding. In all thy ways acknowledge Him, and He shall direct thy paths. Be not wise in thine own eyes: fear the LORD, and depart from evil **(Proverbs 3:5-7)**.*

There are times that Christians may feel like they're in jail, being prisoners in the Lord's cell. We will never get bored if we stay on His (God's) one accord. When we are soldiers in the Lord's camp, there are times that we will have to get our feet damp. Before you get on the Lord's team, He wants you army clean. The Lord will give you direction, and He will also be your protection. You will be in His army with a sword and a shield, when you go out into the field, because you will run into enemies of outrage, and others that want to be saved.

*I THEREFORE, the prisoner of the Lord, beseech you that ye walk worthy of the vocation wherewith ye are called. With all lowliness and meekness, with longsuffering, forbearing one another in love; Endeavouring to keep the unity of the Spirit in the bond of peace **(Ephesians 4:1-3)**. These things have I spoken unto you, that my joy might remain in you, and that your joy might be full **(John 15:11)**. Wherefore take unto you the whole armour of God, that ye may be able to withstand in the evil day, and having done all, to stand. Stand therefore, having your loins girt about with truth, and having on the breastplate of righteousness; And your feet shod with the preparation of the gospel of peace; Above all, taking the shield of faith, wherewith ye shall be able to quench all the fiery darts of the wicked. And take the helmet of salvation, and the sword of the Spirit, which is the word of God **(Ephesians 6:13-17)**: For as the body is one, and hath many members, and all the members of that one body, being many, are one body: so also is Christ. For by one Spirit are we all baptized into one body, whether we be Jews or Gentiles, whether we be bond or free; and have been all made to drink into one Spirit **(I Corinthians 12:12-13)**. He shall cover*

thee with His feathers, and under His wing s shalt thou trust: His truth shall be thy shield and buckler **(Psalm 91:4)**. *Think not that I am come to send peace on earth: I came not to send peace, but a sword* **(Matthew 10:34)**. *The horse is prepared against the day of battle: but safety is of the LORD* **(Proverbs 21:31)**. *For if, when we were enemies, we were reconciled to God by the death of His Son, much more, being reconciled, we shall be saved by His life* **(Romans 5:10)**.

God is alert to your hurts, but He has more mercy when you're planted in His word.

My hands also will I lift up unto thy commandments, which I have loved; and I will meditate in thy statutes. Remember the word unto thy servant, upon which thou hast caused me to hope. This is my comfort in my affliction: for thy word hath quickened me **(Psalms 119:48-50)**.

At the trust level (in the Lord), you will become unbeatable, because you will never quit.

Trust in the Lord with all thine heart; and lean not unto thine own understanding. In all thy ways acknowledge him, and he shall direct thy paths **(Proverbs 3:5-6)**. *Shew me thy ways, O LORD; teach me thy paths. Lead me in thy truth, and teach me: for thou art the God of my salvation; on thee do I wait all the day* **(Psalms 25:4-5)**.

Nothing can beat free, unless it's coming back to me. In Jesus, we put our trust, because He gave His life for us.

For the law of the Spirit of life in Christ Jesus hath made me free from the law of sin and death **(Romans 8:2)**. *Be not as the offence, so also is the free gift. For if through the offence of one many be dead, much more the grace of God, and the gift by grace, which is by one man, Jesus Christ, hath abounded unto many* **(Romans 5:15)**. *For God so loved the world, that He gave His only begotten Son, that whosoever believeth in Him should not perish, but have everlasting life* **(John 3:16)**.

It has been said, "We can do all things through God." But, on the contrary, God can do all things through us.

For it is God which worketh in you both to will and to do of his good pleasure **(Philippians 2:13)**.

If the Lord is our comfort, and we are supposed to make a joyful noise for Him, why then do we make a fearful noise for the adversary to give him joy?

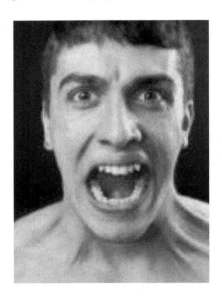

*Make a joyful noise unto God, all ye lands: Sing forth the honour of His name: make his praise glorious (**Psalms 66:1-2**). He restoreth my soul: He leadeth me in the paths of righteousness for His name's sake. Yea, though I walk through the valley of the shadow of death, I will fear no evil: for thou art with me; thy rod and thy staff they comfort me (**Psalms 23:3-4**).*

A student will say to a teacher, "Give me an extra day to do my homework." But, it is God who gives us an extra day every morning that we wake up. If it was me, I would ask if I can turn my work in on the next day or the following day.

> *Be careful for nothing; but in every thing by prayer and supplication with thanksgiving let your requests be made known unto God. And the peace of God, which passeth all understanding, shall keep your hearts and minds through Christ Jesus* **(Philippians 4:6-7)**.

Each trial that we go through, that we don't get credit for on Earth, the Lord will reward us an extra room for our mansion in heaven.

> *Let not your heart troubled: ye believe in God, believe also in Me. In My Father's house are many mansions: if it were not so, I would have told you. I go to prepare a place for you. And if I go and prepare a place for you, I will come again, and receive you unto Myself: that where I am, there ye may be also. And whither I go ye know, and the way ye know* **(John 14:1-4)**. *Beloved, think it not strange concerning the fiery trial which is to try you, as though some strange thing happened unto you: But rejoice, inasmuch as ye are partakers of Christ's sufferings: that, when His glory shall be revealed, ye may be glad also with exceeding joy* **(I Peter 4:12-13)**.

"The Napkin That Knocked Down The Salt Shaker"

There was a man and a woman who went to Waffle House restaurant one afternoon. As they were spicing up their foods, the salt shaker was in the middle of the table. As a napkin slowly landed on the table (after it slipped out of the man's hand), it knocked down the salt shaker.

The man was in complete shock and said, "How did that happen?" I thought about it and said, "The Lord gives us that same power. In the temple of our flesh, we have a mind and a heart. Through meditation and boldness, just like the napkin that knocked down the salt shaker, the Lord gives us that same power to move mountains.

And Jesus said unto them, Because of your unbelief: for verily I say unto you, If ye have faith as a grain of mustard seed, ye shall say unto this mountain, Remove hence to yonder place; and it shall remove; and nothing shall be impossible unto you **(Matthew 17:20)**.

Making a mistake is just a piece of cake. It's just a stepping stone to perfect your trade.

*A wise man will hear, and will increase learning; and a man of understanding shall attain unto wise counsels **(Proverbs 1:5)**: Give instruction to a wise man, and he will be yet wiser: teach a just man, and he will increase in learning **(Proverbs 9:9)**. The steps of a good man are ordered by the LORD: and he delighteth in his way. Though he fall, he shall not be utterly cast down: for the LORD upholdeth him with His hand **(Psalms 37:23-24)**.*

If you speak it into existence, the Lord will bring it into existence. Therefore, if you speak what you want on Earth, the Lord will bring your desires to birth.

*Ask, and it shall be given you; seek, and ye shall find; knock, and it shall be opened unto you: For every one that asketh receiveth; and he that seeketh findeth; and to him that knocketh it shall be opened **(Matthew 7:7-8)**. Therefore I say unto you, What things soever ye desire, when ye pray, believe that ye receive them, and ye shall have them **(Mark 11:24)**. And this is the confidence that we have in Him, that, if we ask any thing according to his will, he heareth us: And if we know that he hear us, whatsoever we ask, we know that we have the petitions that we desired of him **(I John 5:14-15)**. If ye abide in me, and my words abide in you, ye shall ask what ye will, and it shall be done unto you **(John 15:7)**.*

30

True information that transfers to your brain is an enhancement of knowledge gained.

> *Who will have all men to be saved, and to come unto the knowledge of the truth **(I Timothy 2:4)**. And to know the love of Christ, which passeth knowledge, that ye might be filled with all the fulness of God **(Ephesians 3:19)**.*

The bible is like a refrigerator. As you eat and drink from the refrigerator as a child, you will continue to grow. As a child of God hungers, and thirst for the word of God, he/she will continue to eat of the fruit.

> *But he that received seed into the good ground is he that heareth the word, and understandeth it; which also beareth fruit, and bringeth forth, some an hundredfold, some sixty, some thrity* **(Matthew 13:23)**.

Sowing good seed in the field can produce good fruits for healthy spiritual meals.

*And sow the fields, and plant vineyards, which may yield fruits of increase **(Psalm 107:37)**. But he that received seed into the good ground is he that heareth the word, and understandeth it; which also beareth fruit, and bringeth forth, some an hundredfold, some sixty, some thirty. Another parable put he forth unto them, saying, The kingdom of heaven is likened unto a man which sowed good seed in his field **(Matthew 13:23-24)**.*

When you continue to give God the glory, He will change your whole life story.

*And he said, I beseech thee, shew me thy glory. And he said, I will make all my goodness pass before thee, and I will proclaim the name of the LORD before thee; and will be gracious to whom I will be gracious, and will shew mercy on whom I will shew mercy **(Exodus 33:18-19)**.*

Jesus is more than a friend; He's worthy over all men; He died for our sins.

But God commendeth his love toward us, in that, while we were yet sinners, Christ died for us **(Romans 5:8)**. *Greater love hath no man than this, that a man lay down his life for his friends. Ye are my friends, if ye do whatsoever I command you. Henceforth I call you not servants; for the servant knoweth not what his lord doeth: but I have called you friends; for all things that I have heard of my Father I have made known unto you. Ye have not chosen me, but I have chosen you, and ordained you, that ye should go and bring forth fruit, and that your fruit should remain: that whatsoever ye shall ask of the Father in my name, he may give it you* **(John 15:13-16)**. *Saying with a loud voice, Worthy is the Lamb that was slain to receive power, and riches, and wisdom, and strength, and honour, and glory, and blessing. And every*

*creature which is in heaven, and on the earth,
and under the earth, and such as are in the
sea, and all that are in them, heard I saying,
Blessing, and honour, and glory, and power, be
unto him that sitteth upon the throne, and
unto the Lamb for ever and ever*
(Revelations 5:12-13).

Don't believe in the negative, because it
can show disrespect to ourselves in the way
we live.   Therefore, don't let anyone give you
a negative name for what you positively claim.

*A wicked doer giveth heed to false lips; and a liar
giveth ear to a naughty tongue **(Proverbs 17:4)**.
Beloved, believe not every spirit, but try the spirits
whether they are of God: because many false
prophets are gone out into the world. Hereby
know ye the spirit that confesseth not that Jesus
Christ is come in the flesh is of God: And every
spirit that confesseth not that Jesus Christ is come
in the flesh is not of God: and this is that spirit of
an'-ti-christ, whereof ye have heard that it should
come; and even now already is it in the world. Ye
are of God, little children, and have overcome
them: because greater is He that is in you, than
he that is in the world. They are of the world:
therefore speak they of the world, and the world
heareth them **(I John 4:1-5)**.*

There's a thin line between Excel and Fail. A line (-) makes the difference between an E and the F:

Excel   Fail

➢ If you have two questions on a test, and you miss one, you will fail the examination.

➢ If you are having a peaceful conversation with your spouse, and one line is misinterpreted, the conversation may fail, and turn into an argument.

➢ If a building is being built, and one column is removed, the whole building will collapse.

*Hold up my goings in thy paths, that my footsteps slip not **(Psalm 17:5)**. Unless the Lord had been my help, my soul had almost dwelt in silence. When I said, My foot slippeth; thy mercy, O Lord, held me up. In the multitude of my thoughts within me thy comforts delight my soul **(Psalms 94:17-19)**. I will extol thee, O Lord; for thou hast lifted me up, and hast not made my foes to rejoice over me **(Psalm 30:1)**.   Then I saw that wisdom excelleth folly, as far as light excelleth darkness **(Ecclesiastes 2:13)**.*

"Making Every Week/Weak Day Strong"

When the week days arrive, why do we have a tendency of rushing through them by wanting to cut our days and making them weak? We only have one life to live. Why not make each day solid, by doing the best that we can, in this world, and let time take its own twirl. Should we complain when time goes by too fast? We can never go back to the past. Therefore, we should look forward, and stay focused on the future. When we stay busy during the week, the time will go by fast, and when we stay focused on God's purpose for us on Earth, our lives will be solid.

> *Be careful for nothing; but in every thing by prayer and supplication with thanksgiving let your requests be made known unto God* ***(Philippians 4:6)***. *To every thing there is a season, and a time to every purpose under the heaven* ***(Ecclesiastes 3:1)***: *Go to now, ye that say, Today or tomorrow we will go into such a city, and continue there a year, and buy and sell, and get gain: Whereas ye know not what shall be on the morrow. For what is your life? It is even a vapour, that appeareth for a little time, and then vanisheth away* ***(James 4:13-14)***. *Take therefore no thought for the morrow: for the morrow shall take thought for the things of itself. Sufficient unto the day is the evil thereof* ***(Matthew 6:34)***. *Brethren, I count not myself to have apprehended: but this one thing I do, forgetting those things*

*which are behind, and reaching forth unto those things which are before, I press toward the mark for the prize of the high calling of God in Christ Jesus **(Philippians 3:13-14)**. And to know the love of Christ, which passeth knowledge, that ye might be filled with all the fulness of God. Now unto him that is able to do exceeding abundantly above all that we ask or think, according to the power that worketh in us **(Ephesians 3:19-20)**.*

If you can't hush in the spirit of God, you can't be touched by the spirit of God.

*But let it be the hidden man of the heart, in that which is not corruptible, even the ornament of a meek and quiet spirit, which is in the sight of God of great price **(I Peter 3:4)**. But ye are not in the flesh, but in the Spirit, if so be that the Spirit of God dwell in you. Now if any man have not the Spirit of Christ, he is none of his. And if Christ be in you, the body is dead because of sin; but the Spirit is life because of righteousness. But if the Spirit of him that raised up Jesus from the dead dwell in you, he that raised up Christ from the dead shall also quicken your mortal bodies by his Spirit that dwelleth in you. Therefore, brethren, we are debtors, not to the flesh, to live after the flesh. For if ye live after the flesh, ye shall die: but if ye through the Spirit do mortify the deeds of the body, ye shall live. For as many as are led by the Spirit of God, they are the sons of God **(Roman 8:9-14)**.*

37

Those who don't quit will never lose, because their game is not over until they win.

*Not as though I had already attained, either were already perfect: but I follow after, if that I may apprehend that for which also I am apprehended of Christ Jesus. Brethren, I count not myself to have apprehended: but this one thing I do, forgetting those things which are behind, and reaching forth unto those things which are before, I press toward the mark for the prize of the high calling of God in Christ Jesus **(Philippians 3:12-14)**.*

When you change the way you think, the things you think will change.

*For as he thinketh in his heart, so is he: Eat and drink, saith he to thee; but his heart is not with thee **(Proverbs 23:7)**. And be not conformed to this world: but be ye transformed by the renewing of your mind, that ye may prove what is that good, and acceptable, and perfect, will of God **(Romans 12:2)**. Finally, brethren, whatsoever things are true, whatsoever things are honest, whatsoever things are just, whatsoever things are pure, whatsoever things are lovely, whatsoever things are of good report; if there be any virtue, and if there be any praise, think on these things **(Philippians 4:8)**.*

If we as a baby in a crib, has cried out for our parents, here on Earth, to change our diapers, why is it that we are so uptight, and don't want to cry out to our Father in heaven, when He will reach out to change us after we have made a mess?

*But let man and beast be covered with sackcloth, and cry mightily unto God: yea, let them turn every one from his evil way, and from the violence that is in their hands **(Jonah 8:3)**. If we confess our sins, He is faithful and just to forgive us our sins, and to cleanse us from all unrighteousness **(I John 1:9)**.*

Be careful what you speak. It shed's power what you reap.

*He that keepeth his mouth keepeth his life: but he that openeth wide his lips shall have destruction **(Proverbs 13:3)**. Be not deceived; God is not mocked: for whatsoever a man soweth, that shall he also reap **(Galatians 6:7)**.*

39

Satan's words will never line up, his works are to bind you up.

> And that because of false brethren unawares brought in, who came in privily to spy out our liberty which we have in Christ Jesus, that they might bring us into bondage **(Galatians 2:4)**: While they promise them liberty, they themselves are the servants of corruption: for of whom a man is overcome, of the same is he brought in bondage **(II Peter 2:19)**. Stand fast therefore in the liberty wherewith Christ hath made us free, and be not entangled again with the yoke of bondage **(Galatians 5:1)**.

A lady was at work. She was conversing with a couple of her coworkers that were men. She said to them, "I give a man no money." Another man walked over to her and asked, "Ma'am, do you give a man knowledge if he asked you for it?" She answered, "It depends on what kind of knowledge it is." The man replied in return, "Did you know that knowledge is money?"

> For wisdom is a defence, and money is a defence: but the excellency of knowledge is, that wisdom giveth life to them that have it.
> **(Ecclesiastes 7:12)**. But thou shalt remember the LORD thy God: for it is he that giveth thee power to get wealth, that he may establish his covenant which he sware unto thy fathers, as it is this day **(Deuteronomy 8:18)**.

The Lord does not only give us the power to run our own business, but He also gives us the power to run the nations.

And thou say in thine heart, My power and the might of mine hand hath gotten me this wealth. But thou shalt remember the LORD thy God: for it is he that giveth thee power to get wealth, that he may establish his covenant which he sware unto thy fathers, as it is this day **(Deuteronomy 8:17-18)**. *For the LORD thy God blesseth thee, as he promised thee: and thou shalt lend unto many nations, but thou shalt not borrow; and thou shalt reign over many nations, but they shall not reign over thee.* **(Deuteronomy 15:6)**.

In these days, going into a disco dance, you survive by chance, but going into a Holy Ghost party, you can look forward to advance. Before going into that disco dance party, you may have to get patted down, for weapons, and then pay a fee. But, in the Lord's party, you pay your tithing, and not only receive it back through your returns, but you also get other perks for free.

*The joy of our heart is ceased; our dance is turned into mourning. The crown is fallen from our head: woe unto us, that we have sinned (**Lamentations 5:15-16**)! The LORD is my strength and song, and he is become my salvation: he is my God, and I will prepare him an habitation; my father's God, and I will exalt him (**Exodus 15:2**). Bring ye all the tithes into the storehouse, that there may be meat in mine house, and prove me now herewith, saith the LORD of hosts, if I will not open you the windows of heaven, and pour you out a blessing, that there shall not be room enough to receive it. And I will rebuke the devourer for your sakes, and he shall not destroy the fruits of your ground; neither shall your vine cast her fruit before the time in the field, saith the LORD of hosts (**Malachi 3:10-11**).*

Patience is a must, but you can't rely on your lust.

> *This I say then, Walk in the Spirit, and ye shall not fulfil the lust of the flesh. For the flesh lusteth against the Spirit, and the Spirit against the flesh: and these are contrary the one to the other: so that ye cannot do the things that ye would* ***(Galatians 5:16-17)***.

On earth, the sky is the limit. But, God's kingdom is above all skies.

> *Glory to God in the highest, and on earth peace, good will toward men* ***(Luke 2:14)***. *And the kingdom and dominion, and the greatness of the kingdom under the whole heaven, shall be given to the people of the saints of the most High, whose kingdom is an everlasting kingdom, and all dominions shall serve and obey him* ***(Daniel 7:27)***.

When children play most video games, they only ingrain war and combat installed in their brain, in which their emotions can't obtain, so their inner hurt has an outburst of pain.

*I will set no wicked thing before mine eyes: I hate the work of them that turn aside; it shall not cleave to me **(Psalm 101:3)**. Keep thy heart with all diligence; for out of it are the issues of life **(Proverbs 4:23)**. Lest Satan should get an advantage of us: for we are not ignorant of his devices. **(II Corinthians 2:11)**. Watch and pray, that ye enter not into temptation: the spirit indeed is willing, but the flesh is weak **(Matthew 26:41)**. Thou wilt keep him in perfect peace, whose mind is stayed on thee: because he trusteth in thee **(Isaiah 26:3)**.*

We don't have to be good to get good, because God is good, and we have God.

*But now hath he obtained a more excellent ministry, by how much also he is the mediator of a better covenant, which was established upon better promises. For if that first covenant had been faultless, then should no place have been sought for the second. For finding fault with them, he saith, Behold, the days come, saith the Lord, when I will make a new covenant with the house of Israel and with the house of Judah: Not according to the covenant that I made with their fathers in the day when I took them by the hand to lead them out of the land of Egypt; because they continued not in my covenant, and I regarded them not, saith the Lord. For this is the covenant that I will make with the house of Israel after those days, saith the Lord; I will put my laws into their mind, and write them in their hearts: and I will be to them a God, and they shall be to me a people: And they shall not teach every man his neighbour, and every man his brother, saying, Know the Lord: for all shall know me, from the least to the greatest. For I will be merciful to their unrighteousness, and their sins and their iniquities will I remember no more. In that he saith, A new covenant, he hath made the first old. Now that which decayeth and waxeth old is ready to vanish away **(Hebrews 8:6-13)**. But when the fulness of the time was come, God sent forth his Son, made of a woman, made under the law, To redeem them that were under the law, that we might receive the adoption of sons. **(Galatians 4:4-5)**.*

I went to a restaurant one morning so that I could eat breakfast and write my book associated with the Lord's word. A lady walked past my table and saw a lot of papers. She didn't know what I was writing about, nor did she know what I was doing. The lady told me, "You have papers for life!" I replied in return, "That's because many of my writings are coming from the Word Of Life!" (True story)

> *All scripture is given by inspiration of God, and is profitable for doctrine, for reproof, for correction, for instruction in righteousness:* **(II Timothy 3:16)**. *In the beginning was the Word, and the Word was with God, and the Word was God. The same was in the beginning with God. All things were made by him; and without him was not any thing made that was made. In him was life; and the life was the light of men. And the light shineth in darkness; and the darkness comprehended it not* **(John 1:1-5)**. *Remember the word unto thy servant, upon which thou hast caused me to hope. This is my comfort in my affliction: for thy word hath quickened me* **(Psalms 119:49-50)**.

When the devil get in the way of your Plan "A", the Lord will give you a Plan "B", beyond what Satan can see.

> *No weapon that is formed against thee shall prosper; and every tongue that shall rise against thee in judgment thou shalt condemn. This is the heritage of the servants of the LORD, and their righteousness is of me, saith the LORD.* ***(Isaiah 54:17).*** *So shall they fear the name of the LORD from the west, and his glory from the rising of the sun. When the enemy shall come in like a flood, the Spirit of the LORD shall lift up a standard against him* ***(Isaiah 59:19).***

If we are supposed to be the fruit of the spirit, why do people associate the word's "Going Bananas" with going crazy?

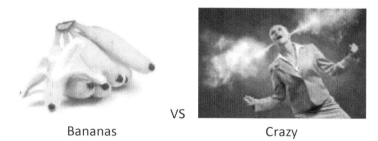

Bananas   VS   Crazy

> *But the fruit of the Spirit is love, joy, peace, longsuffering, gentleness, goodness, faith, Meekness, temperance: against such there is no law* ***(Galatians 5:22-23).*** *Thou wilt keep him in perfect peace, whose mind is stayed on thee: because he trusteth in thee* ***(Isaiah 26:3).***

If your eyes are as a watch, and a watch is as a piece of jewelry, then your body should be treasured as a temple of silver and gold.

Watch =  =

*What? know ye not that your body is the temple of the Holy Ghost which is in you, which ye have of God, and ye are not your own **(I Corinthians 6:19)**? Every man according as he purposeth in his heart, so let him give; not grudgingly, or of necessity: for God loveth a cheerful giver **(II Corinthians 9:7)**.*

He that is first in his own cause, is as he that is first in his own zone.

In other words: In all things that you do, do in the name of the Lord. Don't let your thoughts run your life, but put your trust in the Lord, and have faith in Him. If you try to do everything yourself, in your own power, and leave God out of the equation, He will put you to the test and trial you, by letting you go through tribulations in your own zone.

*He that is first in his own cause seemeth just; but his neighbour cometh and searcheth him **(Proverbs 18:17)**.*

48

Would not you rather take a trip in the air, and be served with a beverage by a flight attendant, and be closer to your Heavenly Father and be blessed, than to trip on your brother or sister in Christ, by attending a fight and stooping to his/her level, where you would fall into his/her mess?

 VS

Keep thy foot when thou goest to the house of God, and be more ready to hear, than to give the sacrifice of fools: for they consider not that they do evil (Ecclesiastes 5:1). For, lo, they that are far from thee shall perish: thou hast destroyed all them that go a whoring from thee. But it is good for me to draw near to God: I have put my trust in the Lord GOD, that I may declare all thy works (Psalms 73:27-28).

If you praise God for the little things, He will amaze you with bigger things.

But seek ye first the kingdom of God, and his righteousness; and all these things shall be added unto you (Matthew 6:33).

How can one claim that they lost something, and get upset, if God is our everything who can restore what we had, to a better form?

> *And the cities which the Philistines had taken from Israel were restored to Israel, from Ekron even unto Gath; and the coasts thereof did Israel deliver out of the hands of the Philistines. And there was peace between Israel and the Amorites **(I Samuel 7:14)**. And I will restore to you the years that the locust hath eaten, the cankerworm, and the caterpiller, and the palmerworm, my great army which I sent among you **(Joel 2:25)**.*

"You Be The King Of Your Castle"

The castle is your body. Don't let Satan come in. Don't let Satan be the crook, and destroy you with his rook. Moreover, don't let him make you into a rookie when you are already made into a castle.

> *What? know ye not that your body is the temple of the Holy Ghost which is in you, which ye have of God, and ye are not your own? For ye are bought with a price: therefore glorify God in your body, and in your spirit, which are God's **(I Corinthians 6:19-20)**. And what agreement hath the temple of God with idols? for ye are the temple of the living God; as God hath said, I will dwell in them, and walk in them; and I will be their God, and they shall be my people **(II Corinthians 6:16)**.*

If we, as Christians are supposed to walk uprightly in the Lord, and our minds determine which path we walk, if our bodies were turned upside down, in which path would we go? Maybe, we wouldn't have a choice, but to stay in one spot, and be prisoners of the Lord, and wait for the gates of Heaven to open for us to be transformed into freedom.

For the LORD God is a sun and shield: the LORD will give grace and glory: no good thing will he withhold from them that walk uprightly.
(Psalm 84:11)*. I therefore, the prisoner of the Lord, beseech you that ye walk worthy of the vocation wherewith ye are called, With all lowliness and meekness, with longsuffering, forbearing one another in love; Endeavouring to keep the unity of the Spirit in the bond of peace* ***(Ephesians 4:1-3)****. And you hath he quickened, who were dead in trespasses and sins; Wherein in time past ye walked according to the course of*

*this world, according to the prince of the power of the air, the spirit that now worketh in the children of disobedience: Among whom also we all had our conversation in times past in the lusts of our flesh, fulfilling the desires of the flesh and of the mind; and were by nature the children of wrath, even as others. But God, who is rich in mercy, for his great love wherewith he loved us, Even when we were dead in sins, hath quickened us together with Christ, (by grace ye are saved;) And hath raised us up together, and made us sit together in heavenly places in Christ Jesus **(Ephesians 2:1-6)**. Now the Lord is that Spirit: and where the Spirit of the Lord is, there is liberty. But we all, with open face beholding as in a glass the glory of the Lord, are changed into the same image from glory to glory, even as by the Spirit of the Lord **(II Corinthians 3:17-18)**.*

Sometimes you will sit where your deeper heart will see something appealing, but in a moment, you will find out that it was all in God's plan for someone to receive healing.

*For I know the thoughts that I think toward you, saith the LORD, thoughts of peace, and not of evil, to give you an expected end. Then shall ye call upon me, and ye shall go and pray unto me, and I will hearken unto you **(Jeremiah 29:11-12)**. Then shall thy light break forth as the morning, and thine health shall spring forth speedily: and thy righteousness shall go before thee; the glory of the LORD shall be thy reward **(Isaiah 58:8)**.*

Jesus died on the cross for our sins. Therefore, because of our sins, the Lord wants us to die from ourselves to crossover. We are already in His image, and now He want us to hold strong to His word so we can mimic.

For God so loved the world, that he gave his only begotten Son, that whosoever believeth in him should not perish, but have everlasting life **(John 3:16)**. *But we all, with open face beholding as in a glass the glory of the Lord, are changed into the same image from glory to glory, even as by the Spirit of the Lord* **(II Corinthians 3:18)**.

If you know who you are in Christ, without doubt, you should never think twice.

For I know the thoughts that I think toward you, saith the LORD, thoughts of peace, and not of evil, to give you an expected end (Jeremiah 29:11). According as he hath chosen us in him before the foundation of the world, that we should be holy and without blame before him in love: Having predestinated us unto the adoption of children by Jesus Christ to himself, according to the good pleasure of his will (Ephesians 1:4-5), For we are his workmanship, created in Christ Jesus unto good works, which God hath before ordained that we should walk in them (Ephesians 2:10). Therefore being justified by faith, we have peace with God through our Lord Jesus Christ: By whom also we have access by faith into this grace wherein we stand, and rejoice in hope of the glory of God (Romans 5:1-2). Ye are all the children of light, and the children of the day: we are not of the night, nor of darkness (I Thessalonians 5:5). Being then made free from sin, ye became the servants of righteousness (Romans 6:18).

If your thoughts are negative, don't rehearse it, because you will open a door for the devil to curse it.

Let this mind be in you, which was also in Christ Jesus: (Philippians 2:5). Thou wilt keep him in perfect peace, whose mind is stayed on thee: because he trusteth in thee (Isaiah 26:3).

When people trip on the floor, there are many times that the person standing will help them up from a wound. Why is it that when people trip on us, as Christians, we refuse to help them up, from a wounded heart? We'd rather feel their hurts, by falling where they fail (to their level), instead of standing our ground to help a brother or sister up (in love), and to let them know who the Lord wants them to stand for.

If someone falls from their ground and go to lower elevations to get a wound, and holler at you, because they see the level that's before their eyes, do not jump to their level and holler right along with them.

*Brethren, if a man be overtaken in a fault, ye which are spiritual, restore such an one in the spirit of meekness; considering thyself, lest thou also be tempted **(Galatians 6:1)**. Now we exhort you, brethren, warn them that are unruly, comfort the feebleminded, support the weak, be patient toward all men **(I Thessalonians 5:14)**. But that on the good ground are they, which in an honest and good heart, having heard the word, keep it, and bring forth fruit with patience **(Luke 8:15)**.*

A couple were about to look up scriptures on the internet through the cell phone. The wife told her husband, "The cell phone might go down and may need to be charged." The husband responded, "Anything that is in the word should not go down. The Lord is charge over all things."

> *Thine, O LORD is the greatness, and the power, and the glory, and the victory, and the majesty: for all that is in the heaven and in the earth is thine; thine is the kingdom, O LORD, and thou art exalted as head above all* **(I Chronicles 29:11)**. *He giveth power to the faint; and to them that have no might he increaseth strength* **(Isaiah 40:29)**.

"Time Is Not Your Friend"

A Pastor once said, "Time is not your friend." When I thought about that, my thoughts expounded on these conclusions:

➢ Time does not wait on you, but a friend does.

➢ In time, we all grow as if time is our mentor because, we all grow in time.

➢ A clock has two hands, and sometimes three (hand in seconds), but it never stops to give us a hand when we are in need, yet, a friend does.

➢ Time counts for itself, so we can't count on time (to wait on us).

➢ Just like a baby, we can't take our eyes off of time; because, you can't depend on time to stay still.

Example: When you close your eyes and go to sleep, time moves so quickly. We awaken from a sleep, and wonder where time has gone.

➢ As children, we claimed some individuals as our friends when they were against us. Time is also against us. As a child gains knowledge through time, time doesn't last forever, and neither does our knowledge. It starts to fade away with time. On that note, can time be as a thief in the night, or perhaps, any parts of the day? A true friend will not still your moment of joy.

Blessed is he that readeth, and they that hear the words of this prophecy, and keep those things which are written therein: for the time is at hand **(Revelation 1:3)**.

"On-The-Ship vs Ownership"

If you are "On-The-Ship", you can only go as far as the ship takes you. But, if you have "Ownership" you have control of how far you will go. Just like in a business, you can only learn the part of the business that is only being taught. On the contrary, if you have ownership in a company, you have no limitations.

> *They that go down to the sea in ships, that do business in great water: And he entered into one of the ships, which was Simon's, and prayed him that he would thrust out a little from the land. And he sat down, and taught the people out of the ship. Now when he had left speaking, he said unto Simon, Launch out into the deep, and let down your nets for a draught. And Simon answering said unto him, Master, we have toiled all the night, and have taken nothing: nevertheless at thy word I will let down the net. And when they had this done, they inclosed a great multitude of fishes: and their net brake* **(Luke 5:3-6)**. *For we are his workmanship, created in Christ Jesus unto good works, which God hath before ordained that we should walk in them* **(Ephesians 2:10)**.

When something appears to go wrong, I've heard the expression, "Suck it up!" Why would you suck up what's not good for your system? I'd rather let it go, and give it to God.

> *Humble yourselves therefore under the mighty hand of God, that he may exalt you in due time: Casting all your care upon him; for he careth for you* **(I Peter 5:6-7)**.

If we are a candle to this world, then Jesus is our brighter half.

> *Ye are the light of the world. A city that is set on an hill cannot be hid. Neither do men light a candle, and put it under a bushel, but on a candlestick; and it giveth light unto all that are in the house. Let your light so shine before men, that they may see your good works, and glorify your Father which is in heaven* **(Matthew 5:14-16)**. *But ye are a chosen generation, a royal priesthood, an holy nation, a peculiar people; that ye should shew forth the praises of him who hath called you out of darkness into his marvellous light* **(I Peter 2:9)**; *Then spake Jesus again unto them, saying, I am the light of the world: he that followeth me shall not walk in darkness, but shall have the light of life* **(John 8:12)**.

When you take charge of your life, you will value yourself. When you value yourself, you can't hold a price with a charge. If you let others value you, they may only put a charge on you that's not worth your value. Your value is life, and life does not hold a price.

> *All things are lawful unto me, but all things are not expedient: all things are lawful for me, but I will not be brought under the power of any* **(I Corinthians 6:12)**. *I will make a man more precious than fine gold; even a man than the golden wedge of O'-phir* **(Isaiah 13:12)**.

"No Debt To Pay"

Jesus reigns Lord of our lives, and Satan is the one who causes strife. The devil has many tricks up his sleeve that he want us to believe. We all should know that he's a liar and a trier, but the Lord our God is our protection, and provider. All we have to do is trust in Him to walk this path that's slim. Our Lord in Heaven, will make it right, we just have to choose Him, who is light of our lives. There are times that we will have to sacrifice, but it will not add up to the price of God's son, Jesus Christ.

> *But he was wounded for our transgressions, he was bruised for our iniquities: the chastisement of our peace was upon him; and with his stripes we are healed **(Isaiah 53:5)**. These six things doth the LORD hate: yea, seven are an abomination unto him: A proud look, a lying tongue, and hands that shed innocent blood, An heart that deviseth wicked imaginations, feet that be swift in running to mischief, A false witness that speaketh lies, and he that soweth discord among brethren **(Proverbs 6:16-19)**. In whom the god of this world hath blinded the minds of them which believe not, lest the light of the glorious gospel of Christ, who is the image of God, should shine unto them **(II Corinthians 4:4)**. But the Lord is faithful, who shall stablish you, and keep you from evil **(II Thessalonians 3:3)**. The LORD shall preserve thee from all evil: he shall preserve thy*

soul. The LORD *shall preserve thy going out and thy coming in from this time forth, and even for evermore **(Psalms 121:7-8)**. Trust in him at all times; ye people, pour out your heart before him: God is a refuge for us. Selah **(Psalm 62:8)**. Then spake Jesus again unto them, saying, I am the light of the world: he that followeth me shall not walk in darkness, but shall have the light of life **(John 8:12)**.*

An ungodly life style may cause a person to be possessed, and if he/she will allow it, that will cause stress.

Blessed is the man that walketh not in the counsel of the ungodly, nor standeth in the way of sinners, nor sitteth in the seat of the scornful. But his delight is in the law of the LORD*; and in his law doth he meditate day and night. And he shall be like a tree planted by the rivers of water, that bringeth forth his fruit in his season; his leaf also shall not wither; and whatsoever he doeth shall prosper. The ungodly are not so: but are like the chaff which the wind driveth away. Therefore the ungodly shall not stand in the judgment, nor sinners in the congregation of the righteous. For the* LORD *knoweth the way of the righteous: but the way of the ungodly shall perish **(Psalms 1:1-6)**. There is therefore now no condemnation to them which are in Christ Jesus, who walk not after the flesh, but after the Spirit **(Romans 8:1)**.*

"Why Walk Around With A Chip On Your Shoulder"

Why is it that people walk around with a chip on their shoulder when the mouth is where it goes? Have their belly run out of space, so they found another storage place? Maybe they didn't want to share and just walk around with a spare. It can be a chip that people want to chew at as they get older, so they'd rather keep that spare weight over their shoulder. Many times we put pressure on ourselves, and that many chips on one shoulder is not good for our health. As we put on our shoulders that much weight, before we know it, we'll be bent out of shape, and sooner or later, we'll break. As it is said that communication is the key, there are times that you have to share your chips with a group, teammate, or family. Pass some of your chips over. In that way, they won't all rest on your shoulder. Aren't many of us putting more on our plates than we can handle? Moreover, are we putting on more than what the plate can handle? If we are stressing from a chip on our shoulder, how long can one stand for a bag of chips? On the contrary, that a bag of chips can put a person into misery before one chip, then I wonder, what are they putting into our food?" Therefore, we should watch what we eat, because what we eat can be the substance of our attitude.

Be ye angry, and sin not: let not the sun go down upon your wrath **(Ephesians 4:26)***: Let all bitterness, and wrath, and anger, and clamour, and evil speaking, be put away from you, with all malice: And be ye kind one to another, tenderhearted, forgiving one another, even as God for Christ's sake hath forgiven you* **(Ephesians 4:31-32)***. Brethren, I count not myself to have apprehended: but this one thing I do, forgetting those things which are behind, and reaching forth unto those things which are before, I press toward the mark for the prize of the high calling of God in Christ Jesus* **(Philippians 3:13-14)***. Remember ye not the former things, neither consider the things of old. Behold, I will do a new thing; now it shall spring forth; shall ye not know it? I will even make a way in the wilderness, and rivers in the desert* **(Isaiah 43:18-19)***. But I keep under my body, and bring it into subjection: lest that by any means, when I have preached to others, I myself should be a castaway* **(I Corinthians 9:27)***. He that hath no rule over his own spirit is like a city that is broken down, and without walls* **(Proverbs 25:28)***.*

It has been said, "Today was a long day, and I'm too tired to do anything else." Why do we complain when time seems to go by so slow? But, we also dance to a slow tune with happiness and joy. We only have one life to live. Enjoy the slow times while you can. On the contrary, we complain when time seems to go by too fast, but we seem to dance to fast music with joy.

> *Neither murmur ye, as some of them also murmured, and were destroyed of the destroyer* **(I Corinthians 10:10)**. *Wherefore, my beloved, as ye have always obeyed, not as in my presence only, but now much more in my absence, work out your own salvation with fear and trembling. For it is God which worketh in you both to will and to do of his good pleasure. Do all things without murmurings and disputings: That ye may be blameless and harmless, the sons of God, without rebuke, in the midst of a crooked and perverse nation, among whom ye shine as lights in the world; Holding forth the word of life; that I may rejoice in the day of Christ, that I have not run in vain, neither laboured in vain* **(Philippians 2:12-16)**. *In every thing give thanks: for this is the will of God in Christ Jesus concerning you* **(I Thessalonians 5:18)**.

When we fight, we will hinder our holy rights, so don't recompense in God's defence.

> *Seeing it is a righteous thing with God to recompense tribulation to them that trouble you; And to you who are troubled rest with us, when the Lord Jesus shall be revealed from heaven with his mighty angels, In flaming fire taking vengeance on them that know not God, and that obey not the gospel of our Lord Jesus Christ: Who shall be punished with everlasting destruction from the presence of the Lord, and from the glory of his power*
> **(2 Thessalonians 1:6-9)**.

The Lord will hear your voice when you call, accept there be any iniquity in your heart, from the Lord's ears, your voice will fall.

> *Hear the voice of my supplications, when I cry unto thee, when I lift up my hands toward thy holy oracle* **(Psalm 28:2)**. *I cried unto him with my mouth, and he was extolled with my tongue. If I regard iniquity in my heart, the Lord will not hear me* **(Psalms 66:17-18)**.

The Lord will never suffer the upright to be moved, so if you cast your cares on him, you won't lose.

> *Cast thy burden upon the LORD, and he shall sustain thee: he shall never suffer the righteous to be moved* **(Psalm 55:22)**.

Never mention that something is hard if you intend to get through it. Only a ghost can go through something hard, but if you have the Spirit of the Holy Ghost, you can do all things through Christ. If you say that something is hard and you depend on the earthly rock, the rock will bounce off of that hard surface. Therefore, believe in Jesus who is our Heavenly Rock, to take you through that which you can't do by yourself.

*And Jesus said unto them, Because of your unbelief: for verily I say unto you, If ye have faith as a grain of mustard seed, ye shall say unto this mountain, Remove hence to yonder place; and it shall remove; and nothing shall be impossible unto you **(Matthew 17:20)**. But without faith it is impossible to please him: for he that cometh to God must believe that he is, and that he is a rewarder of them that diligently seek him **(Hebrews 11:6)**. But Jesus beheld them, and said unto them, With men this is impossible; but with God all things are possible **(Matthew 19:26)**.*

You should always give up, just never let down. In other words: Give up praises where praises are due, and never give power to the devil.

Give thanks unto the LORD, call upon his name, make known his deeds among the people. Sing unto him, sing psalms unto him, talk ye of all his wondrous works. Glory ye in his holy name: let the heart of them rejoice that seek the LORD. Seek the LORD and his strength, seek his face continually **(I Chronicles 16:8-11)**. *Neither give place to the devil* **(Ephesians 4:27)**. *Submit yourselves therefore to God. Resist the devil, and he will flee from you* **(James 4:7)**.

The wicked loves to pick at saints, but the Lord laughs at Satan's drafts. Earth is made for the meek, for us to have peace and not mischief.

But the meek shall inherit the earth; and shall delight themselves in the abundance of peace. The wicked plotteth against the just, and gnasheth upon him with his teeth. The LORD shall laugh at him: for he seeth that his day is coming ***(Psalms 37:11-13).***

If you speak negative from your mouth the situation will become destroyed, but if you allow Jesus to speak through you, the situation won't come back void.

O generation of vipers, how can ye, being evil, speak good things? for out of the abundance of the heart the mouth speaketh. A good man out of the good treasure of the heart bringeth forth good things: and an evil man out of the evil treasure bringeth forth evil things. But I say unto you, That every idle word that men shall speak, they shall give account thereof in the day of judgment. For by thy words thou shalt be justified, and by thy words thou shalt be condemned ***(Matthew 12:34-37)****. For it is not ye that speak, but the Spirit of your Father which speaketh in you* ***(Matthew 10:20).***

Why is it that we depend on others for a handout, when our Father in Heaven has a hand out for us? Is not His hand bigger than ours, here on Earth? Moreover, isn't the world in the palm of His hands?

O my God, I trust in thee: let me not be ashamed, let not mine enemies triumph over me **(Psalm 25:2)**. *Put not your trust in princes, nor in the son of man, in whom there is no help* **(Psalm146:3)**.

When there's a covenant and commitment there should be no quit in it.

What therefore God hath joined together, let not man put asunder **(Mark 10:9)**.

For each trial that we go through, that we don't get credit for on earth, the Lord will reward us an extra room unto our mansion in heaven.

*Let not your heart be troubled: ye believe in God, believe also in me. In my Father's house are many mansions: if it were not so, I would have told you. I go to prepare a place for you. And if I go and prepare a place for you, I will come again, and receive you unto myself; that where I am, there ye may be also. And whither I go ye know, and the way ye know **(John 14:1-4)**. Beloved, think it not strange concerning the fiery trial which is to try you, as though some strange thing happened unto you: But rejoice, inasmuch as ye are partakers of Christ's sufferings; that, when his glory shall be revealed, ye may be glad also with exceeding joy **(I Peter 4:12-13)**.*

There are many times that we don't do what we are supposed to do. Through God, we miss our calling for what we are chosen to do.

*There is one body, and one Spirit, even as ye are called in one hope of your calling **(Ephesians 4:4)**; Let every man abide in the same calling wherein he was called **(I Corinthians 7:20)**.*

God is a good God, He gives us no mess. When we give God His glory, we should give Him our best. What we expect from God, we should give Him no less.

> *Whether therefore ye eat, or drink, or whatsoever ye do, do all to the glory of God* **(I Corinthians 10:31)**.

When people come to a disagreement, often times they become angry, and many have a dispute. It is often said, "I'm going to give you a peace of my mind." I believe that we need our whole mind that God had given us. If you give someone a piece of your mind you will lose it. Another way to emphasize this statement is, "If you give someone a piece of your mind, you will lose peace with yourself."

> *And be renewed in the spirit of your mind; And that ye put on the new man, which after God is created in righteousness and true holiness* **(Ephesians 4:23-24)**. *Thou wilt keep him in perfect peace, whose mind is stayed on thee: because he trusteth in thee* **(Isaiah 26:3)**. *Be ye angry, and sin not: let not the sun go down upon your wrath: Neither give place to the devil* **(Ephesians 4:26-27)**.

We seem to enjoy the amenities of getting online with friends and family, but when it comes to Jesus, and getting on His main line, we miss our calling for the amenities that He has for us.

Thou shalt have no other gods before me. Thou shalt not make unto thee any graven image, or any likeness of any thing that is in heaven above, or that is in the earth beneath, or that is in the water under the earth. Thou shalt not bow down thyself to them, nor serve them: for I the LORD thy God am a jealous God, visiting the iniquity of the fathers upon the children unto the third and fourth generation of them that hate me ***(Exodus 20:3-5)****; Behold, he putteth no trust in his saints; yea, the heavens are not clean in his sight* ***(Job 15:15)****. Trust in the LORD with all thine heart; and lean not unto thine own understanding. In all thy ways acknowledge him, and he shall direct thy paths. Be not wise in thine own eyes: fear the LORD, and depart from evil. It shall be health to thy navel, and marrow to thy bones* ***(Proverbs 3:5-8)****. Who is among you that feareth the LORD, that obeyeth the voice of his servant, that walketh in darkness, and hath no light? let him trust in the name of the LORD, and stay upon his God* ***(Isaiah 50:10)****.*

It's amazing how a minister can throw the word to his/her congregation in a debate for God and some people may feel hurt by what have been thrown at them, and the minister suffers no jail time. But, if an individual were to throw a book at someone in an argument or fight, he/she may suffer jail time for his/her punishment. Isn't the word of God more powerful than any word of any other book, here on Earth?

Pastor throwing God's word at congregation, and receives a church offering.

Person throws a book in an agrument and suffers jail time.

*For the word of God is quick, and powerful, and sharper than any twoedged sword, piercing even to the dividing asunder of soul and spirit, and of the joints and marrow, and is a discerner of the thoughts and intents of the heart **(Hebrews 4:12)**. Be ye angry, and sin not: let not the sun go down upon your wrath: Neither give place to the devil **(Ephesians 4:26-27)**. God, who at sundry times and in divers manners spake in time past unto the fathers by the prophets, Hath in these last days* *spoken unto us by his Son, whom he hath appointed heir of all things, by whom also he made the worlds; Who being the brightness of his glory, and the express image of his person, and upholding all things by the word of his power, when he had by himself purged our sins, sat down on the right hand of the Majesty on high: Being made so much better than the angels, as he hath by inheritance obtained a more excellent name than they* **(Hebrews 1:1-4)**.

A young man came into a restaurant and saw a few thin books about the word of God laying on the counter. He asked, "Are these anyone's books? I just don't want to look like I'm stealing." I responded, "You are supposed to take God's word and run with it every chance you get."

I will run the way of thy commandments, when thou shalt enlarge my heart. Teach me, O Lord, the way of thy statues; and I shall keep it unto the end. Give me understanding, and I shall keep thy law; yea, I shall observe it with my whole heart **(Psalms 119:32-34)**. *Wherefore seeing we also are compassed about with so great a cloud of witnesses, let us lay aside every weight, and the sin which doth so easily beset us, and let us run with patience the race that is set before us. Looking unto Jesus the author and finisher of our faith; who for the joy that was set before Him endured the cross, despising the shame, and is set down at the right hand of the throne of God* **(Hebrews12:1-2)**.

The Lord has laid the foundation of the earth. Why not trust in Him to lay His hands on us, as He wants to mold us in His image? Aren't we a part of the Lord's foundation?

*Mine hand also hath laid the foundation of the earth, and my right hand hath spanned the heavens: when I call unto them, they stand up together **(Isaiah 48:13)**. And God said, Let us make man in our image, after our likeness: and let them have dominion over the fish of the sea, and over the fowl of the air, and over the cattle, and over all the earth, and over every creeping thing that creepeth upon the earth **(Genesis 1:26)**. For we are labourers together with God: ye are God's husbandry, ye are God's building **(I Corinthians 3:9)**. Now he which stablisheth us with you in Christ, and hath anointed us, is God; Who hath also sealed us, and given the earnest of the Spirit in our hearts **(II Corinthians 1:21-22)**.*

It has been said, "It will be my way, or the highway." Me personally, I'd rather take the highway, because my trust is in God, and not man. God is the highway. Moreover, I'd rather take God's way than to put my trust in man.

*The highway leads you
to Heaven*

*Man's Way will lead you
to hell*

*Thus saith the LORD; Cursed be the man that trusteth in man, and maketh flesh his arm, and whose heart departeth from the LORD **(Jeremiah 17:5)**. It is better to trust in the LORD than to put confidence in man **(Psalm 118:8)**.*

Let all things that you say, be positive in the spirit because anything else, the Lord don't want to hear it.

They forgat God their saviour, which had done great things in Egypt; Wondrous works in the land of Ham, and terrible things by the Red sea. Therefore he said that he would destroy them, had not Moses his chosen stood before him in the breach, to turn away his wrath, lest he should destroy them. Yea, they despised the pleasant land, they believed not his word: But murmured in their tents, and hearkened not unto the voice of the LORD. Therefore he lifted up his hand against them, to overthrow them in the wilderness: To overthrow their seed also among the nations, and to scatter them in the lands (Psalms 106:21-27). Do all things without murmurings and disputings (Philippians 2:14): Let no corrupt communication proceed out of your mouth, but that which is good to the use of edifying, that it may minister grace unto the hearers. And grieve not the holy Spirit of God, whereby ye are sealed unto the day of redemption. Let all bitterness, and wrath, and anger, and clamour, and evil speaking, be put away from you, with all malice: And be ye kind one to another, tenderhearted, forgiving one another, even as God for Christ's sake hath forgiven you (Ephesians 4:29-32).

It's funny how someone can be mad or disappointed and say, "I've been set up; or I am upset." But, as Christians, wouldn't you rather be set up on high, and get closer to God, than to be let down by man? Moreover, God is our provider, so why not put your trust in Him?

*God is my strength and power: and he maketh my way perfect. He maketh my feet like hinds' feet: and setteth me upon my high places **(2 Samuel 22:33-34)**. Cease ye from man, whose breath is in his nostrils: for wherein is he to be accounted of **(Isaiah 2:22)**? My soul followeth hard after thee: thy right hand upholdeth me **(Psalm 62:8)**.*

"God Is Alpha, Center, And Omega"

As 1 (One) is the beginning, and 3 (Three) is the ending, the number 2 (two) is the center. Therefore, we arrive to:

1 + 3 = 4 divided by the 2 (Two)
numbers: 1 and 3. Therefore,

$$\frac{4 \text{ (The summation of } 1+3)}{2 \text{ (Total numbers to = sum)}} = 2 \text{ (sum of total numbers} \div \text{ into its sum)}$$

The number 2 is the center of 1 and 3.

We should see God in that same mathematical format.

God is our Alpha and Omega.

The word "And" in mathematical terms means Plus (+).

$$\frac{\text{Alpha} + \text{Omega}}{2} = \frac{\text{Beginning} + \text{End}}{2} = \text{Center}$$

Therefore, God should be the center of our life.

> *And He said unto me, It is done. I am Alpha and Omega, the beginning and end. I will give unto him that is athirst of the fountain of the water of life freely* **(Revelations 21:6-7)**. *I am Alpha and Omega, the beginning and the end, the first and the last* **(Revelation 22:13)**.

A lady was at work. She was conversing with a couple of her co-workers that happen to be men. She said to them, "I give a man no money." Another man walked over to her and asked, "Ma'am, do you give a man knowledge if he asks." She answered, "It depends on what kind of knowledge it is." The man replied, "Did you know that knowledge is money?"

> *For wisdom is a defence, and money is a defence: but the excellency of knowledge is, that wisdom giveth life to them that have it* **(Ecclesiastes 7:12)**. *But thou shalt remember the* LORD *thy God: for it is he that giveth thee power to get wealth, that he may establish his covenant which he sware unto thy fathers, as it is this day* **(Deuteronomy 8:18)**.

There is a saying, "That was the straw that broke the camel's back!" There are many straws to make a block of hay. If that saying is based on what we say, and our actions, we have power in our tongue (for the things we say) and do. On the contrary, if getting over a hump in life will only make you stronger, why break off your challenge that will reap your blessing?

> *For he that soweth to his flesh shall of the flesh reap corruption; but he that soweth to the Spirit shall of the Spirit reap life everlasting. And let us not be weary in well doing: for in due season we shall reap, if we faint not* **(Galatians 6:8-9)**.

Isn't it something how we call a friend's number, to have someone to talk to, when we have a problem, but we don't consider asking the Lord in prayer, about that problem, and waiting for His call, who has a number for every one of us?

> Seek ye the LORD while he may be found, call ye upon him while he is near *(Isaiah 55:6)*. Call unto me, and I will answer thee, and show thee great and mighty things, which thou knowest not *(Jeremiah 33:3)*. For the promise is unto you, and to your children, and to all that are afar off, even as many as the LORD our God shall call *(Acts 2:39)*.

God does not need to change the world, but the people can change. The foundation does not need to be changed, nor does the grounds of the earth, in which we stand on, have a heart.

> He is like a man which built an house, and digged deep, and laid the foundation on a rock: And when the flood arose, the stream beat vehemently upon that house, and could not shake it: for it was founded upon a rock *(Luke 6:48)*. Nevertheless the foundation of God standeth sure, having this seal, The Lord knoweth them that are his. And, let every one that nameth the name of Christ depart from iniquity *(II Timothy 2:19)*. Therefore if any man be in Christ, he is a new creature: old things are passed away; behold, all things are become new *(II Corinthians 5:17)*.

My fiancée and I were out working on a project. I said that I wanted to get a certain amount of information typed before the day comes to an end. She stated, "We might reach that quota." I replied, "The word 'Might' should not be in our vocabulary as true believers. We should know that we can do all things for those who believe." The only time the word "Might" should be used, is when we, as Christians, are referring to strength.

Example of what a Christian shouldn't say:

> ➤ We might be able *to do all things*.

Example of what a Christian should say:

> ➤ The Lord gives us the might *to do all things*.

There are times that we have to turn negatives into positives. We have to add "The Lord" in our equation, to change our whole situation to be positive.

> *I can do all things through Christ which strengtheneth me **(Philippians 4:13)**. Finally, my brethren, be strong in the Lord, and in the power of His might **(Ephesians 6:10)**.*

If there's no us, there's no trust. A "ME" is an upside down "WE".

If "WE" stand on top of the surface, we can work together as a team, and survive in life. But, if "WE" were on the flip side of the water, "WE" would become a "ME". Therefore, if you were under water by yourself (as a "ME" with no help), how long will you be able to survive in life? If you continue to stay under water, without any help in life, will you not drown? Furthermore, if you walked on your hands (being upside down), how far will you go down the road of life without a team to lift you up when you stumble or fall?

*I and my Father are one **(John 10:30)**. There is neither Jew nor Greek, there is neither bond nor free, there is neither male nor female: for ye are all one in Christ Jesus **(Galatians 3:28)**.*

The Lord is looking for us to worship Him. To put this in mathematical terms:

l (in looking) = 1, and
o (in looking) = 0.

Therefore, we arrive to:

The Lord is looking for us to worship Him =

The Lord is 100 King for us to worship Him

Since it is He who has the power,

The Lord = 100% King for us to worship Him.

God is our refuge and strength, a very present help in trouble. Therefore will not we fear, though the earth be removed, and though the mountains be carried into the midst of the sea **(Psalms 46:1-2)**; *Whether therefore ye eat, or drink, or whatsoever ye do, do all to the glory of God* **(I Corinthians 10:31)**. *Which in his times he shall shew, who is the blessed and only Potentate, the King of kings, and Lord of lords; Who only hath immortality, dwelling in the light which no man can approach unto; whom no man hath seen, nor can see: to whom be honour and power everlasting. Amen* **(I Timothy 6:15-16)**.

I hear the term so often, "I can't do nothing right!" Well, you must be doing something right. You see, the term "...can do nothing right!" contradicts "...can't do nothing right!" The words "Can't" and "Nothing" are both negative words in this statement structure.

Coming from a mathematical perspective:

> ➢ Negative (-) X Negative (-) = Positive (+).

But nevertheless, when you have a problem in life:

> ➢ Negative does not X out the other Negative.

It only adds (+) to the problem. Therefore, you have:

> ➢ Negative + Negative = A Deeper Negative.

Therefore, don't dig yourself in a deeper ditch.

*But let him ask in faith, nothing wavering. For he that wavereth is like a wave of the sea driven with the wind and tossed **(James 1:6)**. I can do all things through Christ which strengtheneth me **(Philippians 4:13)**. Recompense to no man evil for evil. Provide things honest in the sight of all men. If it be possible, as much as lieth in you, live peaceably with all men. Dearly beloved, avenge not yourselves, but rather give place unto wrath: for it is written, VENGEANCE IS MINE; I*

WILL REPAY, saith the Lord. Therefore IF THINE ENEMY HUNGER, FEED HIM; IF HE THIRST, GIVE HIM DRINK: FOR IN SO DOING THOU SHALT HEAP COALS OF FIRE ON HIS HEAD. Be not overcome of evil, but overcome evil with good **(Romans 12:17-21)**. *Even so every good tree bringeth forth good fruit; but a corrupt tree bringeth forth evil fruit. A good tree cannot bring forth evil fruit, neither can a corrupt tree bring forth good fruit. Every tree that bringeth not forth good fruit is hewn down, and cast into the fire. Wherefore by their fruits ye shall know them* **(Matthew 7:17-20)**.

Thank the Lord for the sword, because by Satan's demands / demons, we won't stand. Amen?

The snare is laid for him in the ground, and a trap for him in the way **(Job 18:10)**. *Stand therefore, having your loins girt about with truth, and having on the breastplate of righteousness; And your feet shod with the preparation of the gospel of peace; Above all, taking the shield of faith, wherewith ye shall be able to quench all the fiery darts of the wicked. And take the helmet of salvation, and the sword of the Spirit, which is the word of God:* **Ephesians 6:14-17)**. *And ye shall chase your enemies, and they shall fall before you by the sword. And five of you shall chase an hundred, and an hundred of you shall put ten thousand to flight: and your enemies shall fall before you by the sword* **(Leviticus 26:7-8)**.

There was a community called "Heavenly Homes" where a group of people looked at new homes for sale. They were huge mansions. Before the home buyers put the down payment on their homes, they had to make an appointment with a real estate attorney to make sure the homes were appraised. But, I wonder, how much do we keep a-praise up in our Father's house? Moreover, we should keep up our praise in the Lord, whether we are in His house or out.

Blessed shalt thou be when thou comest in, and blessed shalt thou be when thou goest out **(Deuteronomy 28:6)**.

I will bless the LORD at all times: His praise shall continually be in my mouth **(Psalm 34:1)**.

Ye also, as lively stones, are built up a spiritual house, an holy priesthood, to offer up spiritual sacrifices, acceptable to God by Jesus Christ **(1 Peter 2:5)**.

A small speck of black pepper is sprinkled on a plate, in front of you, and it has the power to serve you with a sneeze, before you have the opportunity to chew into it.

Moreover, it will choke you before you knock it down with a punch (beverage). Furthermore, an onion, that is much larger than that tiny speck of black pepper, but is still much smaller than you, has the power to make you cry with a runny nose, when you cut into it.

With that being said: How much more power does God give us over our mountains, if we only have the faith of a mustard seed, which is about the size of a tiny speck of black pepper?

> *If tiny specks of black pepper has the power to season an onion with flavour, and an onion has the power to season the taste of food to flavour, then how much more power does God give us to season our mountains, by His favour, to make them move? Doesn't God give us the power over our mountains for every season that we go through?*

> *And Jesus said unto them, Because of your unbelief: for verily I say unto you, If ye have faith as a grain of mustard seed, ye shall say unto this mountain, Remove hence to yonder place; and it shall remove; and nothing shall be impossible unto you **(Matthew 17:20)**.*

There are times when a cloud will block our light, but God, who is our light, that is above all clouds, will make them move if we will allow Him to fight.

> *The LORD is my light and my salvation; whom shall I fear? the LORD is the strength of my life; of whom shall I be afraid **(Psalm 27:1)**? For the LORD your God is he that goeth with you, to fight for you against your enemies, to save you **(Deuteronomy 20:4)**. And I will bring the blind by a way that they knew not; I will lead them in paths that they have not known: I will make darkness light before them, and crooked things straight. These things will I do unto them, and not forsake them **(Isaiah 42:16)**.*

Isn't it something how we can be free in the Lord and rich in the Lord all at once?

*Then said Jesus to those Jews which believed on Him, If ye continue in my word, then are ye my disciples indeed; And ye shall know the truth, and the truth shall make you free.   They answered Him, We be Abraham's seed, and were never in bondage to any man: how sayest thou, Ye shall be made free? Jesus answered them, Verily, verily, I say unto you, Whosoever committeth sin is the servant of sin. And the servant abideth not in the house for ever: but the Son abideth ever. If the Son therefore shall make you free, ye shall be free indeed **(John 8:31-36)**. The blessings of the LORD, it maketh rich, and He addeth no sorrow with it **(Proverbs 10:22)**. Wealth and riches shall be in His house: and His righteousness endureth for ever **(Psalm 112:3)**.*

When Satan comes to bind you from the *spirit of God, he will rewind you from the spirit of* God. In other words: If you let the devil control your life, you will continue in his circle of unrewarding strifes.

*In whom the god of this world hath blinded the minds of them which believe not, lest the light of the glorious gospel of Christ, who is the image of God, should shine unto them **(II Corinthians 4:4)**.   For God hath not given us the spirit of fear; but of power, and of love, and of a sound mind **(II Timothy 1:7)**. And angry man stirreth up strife, and a furious man aboundeth in transgression **(Proverbs 29:22)**.*

It has been said, "Stop with the excuses." But why stop with excuses instead of leaving them behind us, while we move forward in total truth?

Excuses will get you no where.   *It is better to walk in truth.*

And it came to pass, that, as they went in the way, a certain man said unto him, Lord, I will follow thee whithersoever thou goest. And Jesus said unto him, Foxes have holes, and birds of the air have nests; but the Son of man hath not where to lay his head. And he said unto another, Follow me. But he said, Lord, suffer me first to go and bury my father. Jesus said unto him, Let the dead bury their dead: but go thou and preach the kingdom of God. And another also said, Lord, I will follow thee; but let me first go bid them farewell, which are at home at my house. And Jesus said unto him, No man, having put his hand to the plough, and looking back, is fit for the kingdom of God **(Luke 9:57-62)**.

When the Lord do what He do, what can we do when time is due?

*A man's heart deviseth his way: but the Lord directeth his steps **(Proverbs 16:9)**. To every thing there is a season, and a time to every purpose under the heaven: A time to be born, and a time to die; a time to plant, and a time to pluck up that which is planted; A time to kill, and a time to heal; a time break down, and a time to build up; A time to weep, and a time to laugh; a time to mourn, and a time to dance; A time to cast away stones, and a time to gather stones together; a time to embrace, and a time to refrain from embracing; A time to get, and a time to lose; a time to keep, and a time to cast away; A time to rend, and a time to sew; a time to keep silence, and a time to speak; A time to love, and a time to hate; a time of war, and a time of peace **(Ecclesiastes 3:1-8)**.*

When there is a covenant and a commitment, there should be no quit in it.

*FOR THIS CAUSE SHALL A MAN LEAVE HIS FATHER AND MOTHER, AND CLEAVE TO HIS WIFE; AND THEY TWAIN SHALL BE ONE FLESH: so then they are no more twain, but one flesh. What therefore God hath joined together, let not man put asunder **(Mark 10:7-9)**.*

Shouldn't our hearts be tied onto God's word?

Bind them continually upon thine heart, and tie them about thy neck. When thou goest, it shall lead thee; when thou sleepest, it shall keep thee; and when thou awakest, it shall talk with thee. For the commandment is a lamp; and the law is light; and reproofs of instruction are the way of life **(Proverbs 6:21-23)**.

Your slang is your thang, but My (God's) word is what's heard. In other words, God understands you when you speak His scriptures, and not what's spoken through your lip-terature (literature).

So shall my word be that goeth forth out of my mouth: it shall not return unto me void, but it shall accomplish that which I please, and it shall prosper in the thing whereto I sent it **(Isaiah 55:11)**. *This book of the law shall not depart out thy mouth; but thou shalt meditate therein day and night, that thou mayst observe to do according to all that is written therein: for then thou shalt make thy way prosperous, and then thou shalt have good success* **(Joshua 1:8)**.

Jesus is "The Rock", and He is also my hiding place.

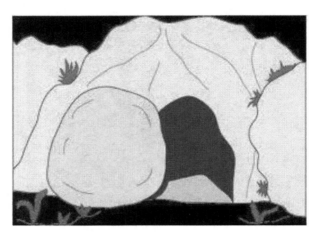

*The Lord is my rock, and my fortress, and my deliverer; my God, my strength, in whom I will trust; my buckler, and the horn of my salvation, and my high tower **(Psalm 18:2)**. For in the time of trouble he shall hide me in his pavilion: in the secret of his tabernacle shall he hide me; he shall set me up upon a rock **(Psalm 27:5)**.*

"Holy" is goal-ly reaching for God, and "Wholly is totally in reach of God.

*And the very God peace sanctify you wholly; and I pray God your whole spirit and soul and body be preserved blameless unto the coming of our Lord Jesus Christ **(1 Thessalonians 5:23)**.*

It's sad how a boss may tell an employee to climb the ladder to get to the top of the company, but at the same time, he/she is looking for that person to slip.

It is better to trust in the LORD than to put confidence in man (Psalm 118:8). Though he fall, he shall not be utterly cast down: for the LORD upholdeth him with his hand (Psalm 37:24).

If you take a test, and from 0% to 100%, you score a 50%, you will fail.

On the contrary, if you speak the words, "I might be able to do that." You just put yourself at a 50% grade. Therefore, why limit yourself to 50%, and why limit yourself by the might (maybe) and might (power) of your thoughts to cause a stronghold on your life? If you take away the maybes by the might of your tongue, you will score higher in life.

> *Death and life are in the power of the tongue: and they that love it shall eat the fruit thereof* ***(Proverbs 18:21)***. *I know thy works, that thou art neither cold nor hot: I would thou wert cold or hot. So then because thou art lukewarm, and neither and neither cold nor hot, I will spue thee out of my mouth* ***(Revelations 3:15-16)***. *No man can serve two masters: for either he will hate the one, and love the other; or else he will hold to the one, and despise the other. Ye cannot serve God and mammon* ***(Matthew 6:24)***.

A lethal weapon is a sword, but the Bible is a legal weapon, which is a sword that we can't ignore.

> *For the word of God is quick, and powerful, and sharper than any twoedged sword, piercing even to the dividing asunder of soul and spirit, and of the joints and marrow, and is a discerner of the thoughts and intents of the heart* ***(Hebrews 4:12)***.

A brother/sister may have a problem in life, where he/she may feel a mental or physical hurt, and the brother/sister (in Christ) may have no problem with teaching them how to overcome that situation, telling them what they were doing wrong, and rehearsing to him/her (over and over about what they did wrong or what they should have done correctly. But, if the brother/sister (in Christ) traded problems with their other brother or sister, would the same rules apply?

Judge not, that ye be not judged. For with what judgment ye judge, ye shall be judged: and with what measure ye mete, it shall be measured to you again. And why beholdest thou the mote that is in thy brother's eye, but considerest not the beam that is in thine own eye? Or how wilt thou say to thy brother, Let me pull out the mote out of thine eye; and, behold, a beam is in thine own eye? Thou hypocrite, first cast out the beam out of thine own eye; and then shalt thou see clearly to cast out the mote out of thy brother's eye **(Matthew 7:1-5)**.

God speaks through man of flesh, the sermon that He knows best.

If any man speak, let him speak as the oracles of God; if any man minister, let him do it as of the ability which God giveth: that God in all things may be glorified through Jesus Christ, to whom be praise and dominion for ever and ever. A-men' **(I Peter 4:11)**.

The Bible is a shield of protection for the darts of evil that are thrown against us.

Wherefore take unto you the whole armour of God, that ye may be able to withstand in the evil day, and having done all, to stand. Stand therefore, having your loins girt about with truth, and having on the breastplate of righteousness; And your feet shod with the preparation of the gospel of peace; Above all, taking the shield of faith, wherewith ye shall be able to quench all the fiery darts of the wicked. And take the helmet of salvation, and the sword of the Spirit, which is the word of God **(Ephesians 6:16-17)**.

In a relationship, if you aren't in one ac/cord, then you may be in for an elect/trick (electric) shock that you can't afford.

In a transaction, when you ask for money to be wired, and the wire details does not match your request, are you not in shock?

*Giving thanks always for all things unto God and the Father in the name of our Lord Jesus Christ; Submitting yourselves one to another in the fear of God. Wives, submit yourselves unto your own husbands, as unto the Lord. For the husband is the head of the wife, even as Christ is the head of the church: and he is the saviour of the body. Therefore as the church is subject unto Christ, so let the wives be to their own husbands in every thing. Husbands, love your wives, even as Christ also loved the church, and gave himself for it **(Ephesians 5:20-25)**; Lest Satan should get an advantage of us: for we are not ignorant of his devices **(2 Corinthians 2:11)**.*

Most of us have heard that the price is right. But, have you ever considered "The Price Is Christ"? On the flipside, "Christ Is Right".

*What? Know ye not that your body is the temple of the Holy Ghost which is in you, which ye have of God, and ye are not your own **(I Corinthians 6:19-20)**? But God commendeth his love toward us, in that, while we were yet sinners, Christ died for us **(Romans 5:8)**.*

It is said that the bible is a coded book. If you can't find the code, then how can you win over souls (to Christ)?

*The fruit of the righteous is a tree of life; and he that winneth souls is wise **(Proverbs 11:30)**. Go ye therefore, and teach all nations, baptizing them in the name of the Father, and of the Son, and of the Holy Ghost: Teaching them to observe all things whatsoever I have commanded you: and lo, I am with you always, even unto the end of the world. Amen **(Matthew 28:19-20)**.*

Pencil can erase, but ink can't unlace. Therefore, write your plan in ink to make it distinct.

> *My heart is inditing a good matter: I speak of the things which have made touching the king: my tongue is the pen of a ready writer* **(Psalm 45:1)**. *And the LORD answered me, and said, Write the vision, and make it plain upon tables, that he may run that readeth it. For the vision is yet for an appointed time, but at the end it shall speak, and not lie: though it tarry, wait for it; because it will surely come, it will not tarry* **(Habakkuk 2:2-3)**. *Be careful for nothing; but in every thing by Prayer and supplication with thanksgiving let your requests be made known unto God* **(Philippians 4:6)**.

It's something how a criminal can be charged with a battery, and be electrocuted from a higher power (in the electric chair) for life. But, will not you be dead from this world and charged by our Lord (God), who never runs out of electric currents?

> *And I saw the dead, small and great, stand before God; and the books were opened: and another book was opened, which is the book of life: and the dead were judged out of those things which were written in the books, according to their works* **(Revelation 20:12)**. *For the wages of sin is death; but the gift of God is eternal life through Jesus Christ our Lord* **(Romans 6:23)**.

A back track don't always mean slack. It also means being assured before moving forward.

> *Let the wick forsake his way, and the righteous man his thoughts: and let him return unto the LORD, and he will have mercy upon him; and to our God, for he will abundantly pardon **(Isaiah 55:7)**. And I will give them an heart to know me, that I am the LORD: and they shall be my people, and I will be their God: for they shall return unto me with their whole heart **(Jeremiah 24:7)**. And hereby we know that we are of the truth, and shall assure our hearts before him. For if our heart condemn us, God is greater than our heart, and knoweth all things. Beloved, if our heart condemn us not, then have we confidence toward God. And whosoever we ask, we receive of him, because we keep his commandments, and do those things that are pleasing in his sight **(1 John 3:19-22)**.*

If you'll move Me (God) by your move, I'll (God) move you.

> *When a man's ways please the LORD, He maketh even his enemies to be at peace with him **(Proverbs 16:7)**. But without faith it is impossible to please Him: for he that cometh to God must believe that He is, and that He is a rewarder of them that diligently seek Him **(Hebrews 11:6-7)**.*

Jesus died on the cross for our lives, and the devil wants to try and stop us every chance he gets. When you go up or down the block (that tries to keep you in bondage), isn't there a crossroad at the end of each block? Furthermore, is not each crossroad covered with stripes?

Each of us has a role/road in life, but the pavements may be bumpy at times. We also have hills that gives us ups and downs. But, are we not healed by Jesus' stripes? Moreover, when we go to the waters (perhaps the sea) to get baptized, is there a block? You cannot live in a block where a home sits on top of the waters, but the waters can give us life over all the nations, were Satan can't give you blockage from God's anointing.

Who his own self bare our sins in his own body on the tree, that we, being dead to sins, should live unto righteousness: BY WHOSE STRIPES YE WERE HEALED **(1 Peter 2:24)**. *But he was wounded for our transgressions, he was bruised for our iniquities' the chastisement of our peace was upon him: and with his stripes we are healed* **(Isaiah 53:5)**. *Stand fast therefore in the liberty wherewith Christ hath made us free, and be not entangled again with the yoke of bondage* **(Galatians 5:1)**. *Thou wilt shew me the path of life: in thy presence is fulness of joy; at thy right hand there are pleasures for evermore* **(Psalm 16:11)**. *And shall say, Cast ye up, cast ye up, prepare the way, take up the stumblingblock out of the way of my people* **(Isaiah 57:14)**.

When a person is being prayed over by one person (at that moment) through prophecy, for that one issue, should a person have two different stories being manifested to him/her for the same issue? Are you not hurt enough from the first prophecy, so you find the need to go to someone else for a second <u>man</u>-ife-<u>story</u>? The only time that more than one person should pray for you, is if they were coming together/to gather into agreement. In some books, isn't there two or three authors that come together in one story? But, if you get knocked down by the spirit, from two different stories, will you not be confused? Moreover, if you were in a two story apartment building, and you fell from the first story, you may feel some hurt. If you fell from the second story, will you not be injured? If you don't have trust in a man of God to pray for you, why go to two?

*And all things, whatsoever ye shall ask in prayer, believing, ye shall receive **(Matthew 21:22)**. Verily I say unto you, Whatsoever ye shall bind on earth shall be bound in heaven: and whatsoever ye shall loose on earth shall be loosed in heaven. Again I say unto you, That if two of you shall agree on earth as touching any thing that they shall ask, it shall be done for them of my Father which is in heaven. For where two or three are gathered together in my name, there am I in the midst of them **(Matthew 18:18-20)**. So then faith cometh by hearing, and hearing by the word of God **(Romans 10:17)**. Now faith is the* *substance of things hoped for, the evidence of things not seen (**Hebrews11:1**). But without faith it is impossible to please him: for he that cometh to God must believe that he is, and that he is a rewarder of them that diligently seek him (**Hebrews 11:6**).*

There is a saying, "I'm under the weather." If God has control over the weather, doesn't He have control over all men?

*There are many devices in a man's heart; nevertheless the counsel of the LORD, that shall stand (**Proverbs 19:21**). But our God is in the heavens: he hath done whatsoever he hath pleased (**Psalm 115:3**). In whom also we have obtained an inheritance, being predestinated according to the purpose of him who worketh all things after the counsel of his own will (**Ephesians 1:11**): In all thy ways acknowledge him, and he shall direct thy paths (**Proverbs 3:6**).*

Jesus' blood pours as an ocean of life. His blood is freshly manufactured on bibles today.

*And being in an agony he prayed more earnestly: and his sweat was as it were great drops of blood falling down to the ground (**Luke 22:44**). And he said unto them, This is my blood of the new testament, which is shed for many (**Mark 14:24**).*

Isn't it funny how a teacher would use a red ink pen to mark wrong answers on a test, but when Jesus speaks throughout the bible in the new test-a-ment, His markings are in red? Isn't the knowledge that Jesus ministers to us in truth? Moreover, isn't He the teacher of all teachers?

Jesus saith unto him, I am the way, the truth, and the life: no man cometh unto the Father, but by me **(John 14:6)**. *My brethren, be not many masters, knowing that we shall receive the greater condemnation. For in many things we offend all. If any man offend not in word, the same is a perfect man, and able also to bridle the whole body* **(James 3:1-2)**. *Whosoever transgresseth, and abideth not in the doctrine of Christ, hath not God. He that abideth in the doctrine of Christ, he hath both the Father and the Son* **(2 John 1:9)**. *The same came to Jesus by night, and said unto him, Rabbi, we know that thou art a teacher come from God: for no man can do these miracles that thou doest, except God be with him* **(John 3:2)**. *And Jesus went about all Galilee, teaching in their synagogues, and preaching the gospel of the kingdom, and healing all manner of sickness and all manner of disease among the people* **(Matthew 4:23)**. *For he taught them as one having authority, and not as the scribes* **(Matthew 7:29)**.

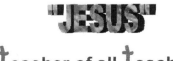

†eacher of all †eachers

2 CHAPTER

PLAY ON WORDS

When Satan gives you a negative opportunity, God can change it for a swapportunity.

> *And Joseph said unto them, Fear not: for am I in the place of God? But as for you, ye thought evil against me; but God meant it unto good, to bring to pass, as it is this day, to save much people alive* **(Genesis 50:19-20)**.

The Lord has a will to do all great things. Therefore, all great things the Lord will do. Since the Lord has a will to do all great things, He passes His will to you.

> *I would seek unto God, and unto God would I commit my cause: Which doeth great things and unsearchable; marvellous things without number* **(Job 5:8-9)**. *The LORD hath done great things for us; whereof we are glad* **(Psalm 126:3)**. *O LORD, how great are thy works! and thy thoughts are very deep* **(Psalm 92:5)**. *All that the Father giveth me shall come to me; and him that cometh to me I will in no wise cast out. For I came down from heaven, not to do mine own will, but the will of him that sent me* **(John 6:37-38)**.

If God be for us, who can be against us? Therefore, if God is before us, who can be after us? No one but God. God is our Alpha and Omega.

> *And we know that all things work together for good to them that love God, to them who are the called according to his purpose. Moreover whom he did predestinate, them he also called: and whom he called, them he also justified: and whom he justified, them he also glorified. What shall we then say to these things? If God be for us, who can be against us* ***(Romans 8:28-31)****?*

The Lord draws attention to those who wants to be saved, but He wants everyone in the picture who comes to Him.

> *My son, attend to my words; incline thine ear unto my sayings* ***(Proverbs 4:20)****. Till I come, give attendance to reading, to exhortation, to doctrine. Neglect not the gift that is in thee, which was given thee by prophecy, with the laying on of the hands of the presbytery. Meditate upon these things; give thyself wholly to them; that thy profiting may appear to all. Take heed unto thyself, and unto the doctrine; continue in them: for in doing this thou shalt both save thyself, and them that hear thee* ***(I Timothy 4:13-16)****. Therefore with joy shall ye draw water out of the wells of salvation* ***(Isaiah 12:3)****.*

The Lord can change your ways of gossip, and strengthen you through His God-sip.

> *For he that will love life, and see good days, let him refrain his tongue from evil, and his lips that they speak no guile* **(I Peter 3:10)**. *The wicked is snared by the transgression of his lips: but the just shall come out of trouble. A man shall be satisfied with good by the fruit of his mouth: and the recompence of a man's hands shall be rendered unto him* **(Proverbs 12:13-14)**.

He that findeth his peace findeth a good piece in life. His peace is referred to as his wife, and piece is referred to as a part of him.

> *Ask, and it shall be given you; seek, and ye shall find; knock, and it shall be opened unto you* **(Matthew 7:7)**. *Whoso findeth a wife findeth a good thing, and obtaineth favour of the* LORD **(Proverbs 18:22)**.

You have to watch how you Twit (treat) yourself because others will Twit (treat) you the same way.

> *Therefore all things whatsoever ye would that men should do to you, do ye even so to them: for this is the law and the prophets* **(Matthew 7:12)**.

One day, I showed my skills to a customer. She told me to never give up at what I do. I said in return, "I always give up to where praises are due, because it's God who pulls me through. I just never let down."

A man's gift maketh room for him, and bringeth him before great men **(Proverbs 18:16)**. *But thanks be to God, which giveth us the victory through our Lord Jesus Christ. Therefore, my beloved brethren, be ye stedfast, unmoveable, always abounding in the work of the Lord, forasmuch as ye know that your labour is not in vain in the Lord* **(I Corinthians 15:57-58)**.

As a Christian, I will have enemies, but I can't let them get in-to-me.

I will keep thy statutes: O forsake me not utterly **(Psalm 119:8)**. *When a man's ways please the LORD, he maketh even his enemies to be at peace with him* **(Proverbs 16:7)**.

Pray and don't worry. Don't worry and pray.

*Casting all your care upon him; for he careth for you (**I Peter 5:7**). Be careful for nothing; but in every thing by prayer and supplication with thanksgiving let your requests be made known unto God. And the peace of God, which passeth all understanding, shall keep your hearts and minds through Christ Jesus (**Philippians 4:6-7**).*

Oftentimes weather reporters predict what the weather is going to be, they are not always on key. Only the Lord's predictions are right.

*And he said unto them, Where is your faith? And they being afraid wondered, saying one to another, What manner of man is this! for he commandeth even the winds and water, and they obey him (**Luke 8:25**). And I will make them and the places round about my hill a blessing; and I will cause the shower to come down in his season; there shall be showers of blessing (**Ezekiel 34:26**).*

If "u" were upside down, "u" would come to an "n" which could stand for "nothing." Therefore, God's creation is for "u" to stand for something.

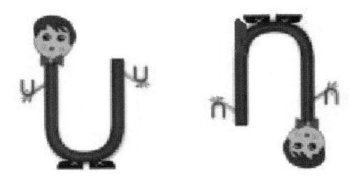

On the contrary, let's put "i" in the place of "u": If "i" were upside down, "i" would become an exclamation point (!). Look at the dot as a person's head, and the line as the body.

If "i" were upside down for too long, "i" would become a question mark (?), like a loss of balance.

People would wonder as wonders with questions. Therefore, "i" stand for something. Don't let people turn you around!

y o u   n o ʎ

*Don't let people turn **you** into a **noT**, or you will be noT for good. In this illustration, "**noT** for good" is referred to as **noT** in replacement for good. But, God has formed us to be good instead of a **noT**.*

*Furthermore, if you were turned into a **K(noT)**, would you get a loose from bondage?*

It's something how one can hear the message read and get one perspective, and read the message for themselves, and see it from the flip side.

*Therefore, my beloved brethren, be ye stedfast, unmoveable, always abounding in the work of the Lord, forasmuch as ye know that your labour is not in vain in the Lord **(I Corinthians 15:58)**.*

If you were my watch, and I see you in time, will you be my treasure?

*For where your treasure is, there will your heart be also **(Matthew 6:21)**. The statutes of the LORD are right, rejoicing the heart: the commandment of the LORD is pure, enlightening the eyes. The fear of the LORD is clean, enduring for ever: the judgments of the LORD are true and righteous altogether. More to be desired are they than gold, yea, than much fine gold: sweeter also than honey and the honeycomb **(Psalms 19:8-10)**. Set a watch, O LORD, before my mouth; keep the door of my lips. Incline not my heart to any evil thing, to practise wicked works with men that work iniquity: and let me not eat of their dainties. Let the righteous smite me; it shall be a kindness: and let him reprove me; it shall be an excellent oil, which shall not break my head: for yet my prayer also shall be in their calamities **(Psalms 141:3-5)**.*

My fiancé told me to trade seats so she can keep an eye on the time. I asked her, "You don't trust me with the time?" She replied, "No!" You are good with numbers, but you can't tell time." I replied, "I can't tell time, because time doesn't listen, because when you tell time to stop, it keeps running."

It's funny how we try to kill time by doing other things, like ringing it during an alarm. But, time still seems to get away.

*And he said unto them, It is not for you to know the times or the seasons, which the Father hath put in his own power **(Acts 1:7)**.*

If you don't make sense/cents, you can't make change, and if you can't make change, you won't make profit.

*There is treasure to be desired and oil in the dwelling of the wise; but a foolish man spendeth it up **(Proverbs 21:20)**.*

With little sense/cents, you can make a lot of change. It just depends on how you install it and invest it, using your brain.

*And he had in his hand a little book open: and he set his right foot upon the sea, and his left foot on the earth **(Revelation 10:2)**. But the manifestation of the Spirit is given to every man to profit withal **(I Corinthians 12:7)**. Thus saith the LORD, thy Redeemer, the Holy One of Israel; I am the LORD thy God which teacheth thee to profit, which leadeth thee by the way that thou shouldest go **(Isaiah 48:17)**. And thou shalt bestow that money for whatsoever thy soul lusteth after, for oxen, or for sheep, or for wine, or for strong drink, or for whatsoever thy soul desireth: and thou shalt eat there before the LORD thy God, and thou shalt rejoice, thou, and thine household **(Deuteronomy 14:26)**. Bring ye all the tithes into the storehouse, that there may be meat in mine house, and prove me now herewith, saith the LORD of hosts, if I will not open you the windows of heaven, and pour you out a blessing, that there shall not be room enough to receive it. And I will rebuke the devourer for your sakes, and he shall not destroy the fruits of your ground; neither shall your vine cast her fruit before the time in the field, saith the LORD of hosts **(Malachi 3:10-11)**.*

Let the Lord be your will/wheel, because He will drive you in the right direction.

*Search me, O God, and know my heart: try me, and know my thoughts: And see if there be any wicked way in me, and lead me in the way everlasting **(Psalms 139:23-24)**. He restoreth my soul: he leadeth me in the paths of righteousness for his name's sake **(Psalm 23:3)**. For it is God which worketh in you both to will and to do of his good pleasure **(Philippians 2:13)**. And the world passeth away, and the lust thereof: but he that doeth the will of God abideth for ever **(I John 2:17)**.*

It's about time change has come, and change has come through time.

*To every thing there is a season, and a time to every purpose under the heaven **(Ecclesiastes 3:1)**.*

When we eat, we taste how our food is seasoned, and for every season, we eat of God's word.

*And they, continuing daily with one accord in the temple, and breaking bread from house to house, did eat their meat with gladness and singleness of heart **(Acts 2:46)**. O taste and see that the LORD is good: blessed is the man that trusteth in him **(Psalm 34:8)**.*

Jesus will never be apart from your life, but He will always be a part of your life.

*Let your conversation be without covetousness; and be content with such things as ye have: for he hath said, I will never leave thee, nor forsake thee. So that we may boldly say, The Lord is my helper, and I will not fear what man shall do unto me **(Hebrews 13:5-6)**. Be strong and of a good courage, fear not, nor be afraid of them: for the LORD thy God, he it is that doth go with thee; he will not fail thee, nor forsake thee **(Deuteronomy 31:6)**.*

It's something how the activities of many children have changed. They used to have a great time playing "Hopscotch." These days, they leave out the hopping and go straight to the Scotch.

Girl jump hopscotch.   *Boy leaves out the Hop and goes straight for the Scotch.*

Train up a child in the way he should go: and when he is old, he will not depart from it **(Proverbs 22:6)**.

God draws all Christians to His attention, but, He welcomes sinners to His picture, who wants to be saved.

Submit yourselves therefore to God. Resist the devil, and he will flee from you. Draw nigh to God, and he will draw nigh to you. Cleanse your hands, ye sinners; and purify your hearts, ye double minded **(James 4:7-8)**.

We should treat the Bible as a car, because it gives you drive.

For(war)d Christ(ler)

When we let God work through our hands and minds, the anointed product will make a name for itself.

But be ye doers of the word, and not hearers only, deceiving your own selves. For if any be a hearer of the word, and not a doer, he is like unto a man beholding his natural face in a glass: For he beholdeth himself, and goeth his way, and straightway forgetteth what manner of man he was. But whoso looketh into the perfect law of liberty, and continueth therein, he being not a forgetful hearer, but a doer of the work, this man shall be blessed in his deed. If any man among you seem to be religious, and bridleth not his tongue, but deceiveth his own heart, this man's religion is vain (James 1:22-26).

We have to do more than just see the test,
but there are times that we have to test the sea.

Don't just see the test.   *Test the sea.*

*Who opposeth and exalteth himself above all that is called God, or that is worshipped; so that he as God sitteth in the temple of God, shewing himself that he is God **(II Thessalonians 2:4)**. Beloved, think it not strange concerning the fiery trial which is to try you, as though some strange thing happened unto you: But rejoice, inasmuch as ye are partakers of Christ's sufferings; that, when his glory shall be revealed, ye may be glad also with exceeding joy. If ye be reproached for the name of Christ, happy are ye; for the spirit of glory and of God resteth upon you: on their part he is evil spoken of, but on your part he is glorified. But let none of you suffer as a murderer, or as a thief, or as an evildoer, or as a busybody in other men's matters. Yet if any man suffer as a Christian, let him not be ashamed; but let him glorify God on this behalf **(I Peter 4:12-16)**. God is our refuge and strength, a very present help in trouble. Therefore will not we fear, though the earth be removed, and though the mountains* *be carried into the midst of the sea; Though the waters thereof roar and be troubled, though the mountains shake with the swelling thereof. Selah. There is a river, the streams whereof shall make glad the city of God, the holy place of the tabernacles of the most High **(Psalms 46:1-4)**. And it shall be in that day, that living waters shall go out from Jerusalem; half of them toward the former sea, and half of them toward the hinder sea: in summer and in winter shall it be **(Zechariah 14:8)**. And the LORD spake unto Moses, Say unto Aaron, Take thy rod, and stretch out thine hand upon the waters of Egypt, upon their streams, upon their rivers, and upon their ponds, and upon all their pools of water, that they may become blood; and that there may be blood throughout all the land of Egypt, both in vessels of wood, and in vessels of stone. And Moses and Aaron did so, as the LORD commanded; and he lifted up the rod, and smote the waters that were in the river, in the sight of Pharaoh, and in the sight of his servants; and all the waters that were in the river were turned to blood **(Exodus 7:19-20)**.*

If you have a piece of God, you will have peace with God.

*My flesh and my heart faileth: but God is the strength of my heart, and my portion for ever **(Psalm 73:26)**. Therefore being justified by faith, we have peace with God through our Lord Jesus Christ **(Romans 5:1)**.*

Are you an eyewitness for the Lord, or are you an "I" witness for the Lord.

Eyewitness: *That which was from the beginning, which we have heard, which we have seen with our eyes, which we have looked upon, and our hands have handled, of the Word of life; For the life was manifested, and we have seen it, and bear witness, and shew unto you that eternal life, which was with the Father, and was manifested unto us **(I John 1:1-2)**. And he turned him unto his disciples, and said privately, Blessed are the eyes which see the things that ye see **(Luke 10:23)**. And the Father himself, which hath sent me, hath borne witness of me. Ye have neither heard his voice at any time, nor seen his shape **(John 5:37)**.*

Eyewitness

I Witness: *But as it is written, Eye hath not seen, nor ear heard, neither have entered into the heart of man, the things which God hath prepared for them that love him. But God hath revealed them unto us by his Spirit: for the Spirit searcheth all things, yea, the deep things of God* **(I Corinthians 2:9-10)**. *The Spirit itself beareth witness with our spirit, that we are the children of God* **(Romans 8:16)**.

"I" Witness

People can be a persecution/person-cution, and they will send/sin you places that you don't want to go.

Yea, and all that will live godly in Christ Jesus shall suffer persecution. But evil men and seducers shall wax worse and worse, deceiving, and being deceived **(II Timothy 3:12-13)**.

We seem to abide by man's rules to conquer the job as a bookkeeper, but why do we find it so hard to abide by the Lord's rules as a word keeper? Isn't it more challenging to pick up a stone than it is a rock? Jesus is "The Rock". It also seems much easier to lift up "The Rock" in praise than a stone.

*It's easier to lift "The Rock" up in praise
than it is a stone.*

*Then said Jesus to those Jews which believed on him, If ye continue in my word, then are ye my disciples indeed **(John 8:31)**. Then Peter and the other apostles answered and said, We ought to obey God rather than men. **(Acts 5:29)**. Put them in mind to be subject to principalities and powers, to obey magistrates, to be ready to every good work **(Titus 3:1)**. For that which I do I allow not: for what I would, that do I not; but what I hate, that do I **(Romans 7:15)**. A stone is heavy, and the sand weighty; but a fool's wrath is heavier than them both **(Proverbs 27:3)**. Because thy lovingkindness is better than life, my lips shall praise thee **(Psalm 63:3)**. And David spake unto* *the LORD the words of this song in the day that the LORD had delivered him out of the hand of all his enemies, and out of the hand of Saul: And he said, The LORD is my rock, and my fortress, and my deliverer* **(II Samuel 22:1-2)**.

You shouldn't say what you don't want to see, because you see what you say.

Death and life are in the power of the tongue: and they that love it shall eat the fruit thereof **(Proverbs 18:21)**. *O generation of vipers, how can ye, being evil, speak good things? for out of the abundance of the heart the mouth speaketh* **(Matthew 12:34)**.

When people trip, give them your hand to help them up again.

Recompense to no man evil for evil. Provide things honest in the sight of all men. If it be possible, as much as lieth in you, live peaceably with all men. Dearly beloved, avenge not yourselves, but rather give place unto wrath: for it is written, Vengeance is mine; I will repay, saith the Lord. Therefore if thine enemy hunger, feed him; if he thirst, give him drink: for in so doing thou shalt heap coals of fire on his head. Be not overcome of evil, but overcome evil with good **(Romans 12:17-21)**.

God reigns Lord of our life, and it is God who gives us rain.

God reigns Lord.   *God gives us rain.*

*God reigneth over the heathen: God sitteth upon the throne of his holiness **(Psalm 47:8)**. Who giveth rain upon the earth, and sendeth waters upon the fields: To set up on high those that be low; that those which mourn may be exalted to safety **(Job 5:10-11)**.*

In Jesus, the victory is won; and we are also one in the Lord.

*There is neither Jew nor Greek, there is neither bond nor free, there is neither male nor female: for ye are all one in Christ Jesus **(Galatians 3:28)**. But thanks be to God, which giveth us the victory through our Lord Jesus Christ **(I Corinthians 15:57)**.*

All individuals on earth have a purpose. The Lord gave us all talents. Therefore, we all have a business. Every organization should have an account. The Lord should be our account. Why not bank on "Him," and let "Him" be our trust?

> *Grant thee according to thine own heart, and fulfil all thy counsel* **(Psalm 20:4)**. *If thou count me therefore a partner, receive him as myself. If he hath wronged thee, or oweth thee ought, put that on mine account* **(Philemon 1:17-18)**. *Cease ye from man, whose breath is in his nostrils: for wherein is he to be accounted of* **(Isaiah 2:22)**? *But I trusted in thee, O LORD: I said, Thou art my God* **(Psalm 31:14)**. *With thy wisdom and with thine understanding thou hast gotten thee riches, and hast gotten gold and silver into thy treasures* **(Ezekiel 28:4)**.

God wants us to have a piece of His word every day, and every day, through God's word, He wants us to have peace.

> *Study to shew thyself approved unto God, a workman that needeth not to be ashamed, rightly dividing the word of truth* **(II Timothy 2:15)**. *And let the peace of God rule in your hearts, to the which also ye are called in one body; and be ye thankful. Let the word of Christ dwell in you richly in all wisdom; teaching and admonishing one another in psalms and hymns and spiritual songs, singing with grace in your hearts to the Lord* **(Colossians 3:15-16)**.

Leave your frustrations there, and don't take another stair/stare.

*And Jesus said unto him, No man, having put his hand to the plough, and looking back, is fit for the kingdom of God **(Luke 9:62)***. *For yet a little while, and he that shall come will come, and will not tarry. Now the just shall live by faith: but if any man draw back, my soul shall have no pleasure in him. But we are not of them who draw back unto perdition; but of them that believe to the saving of the soul* **(Hebrews 10:37-39)**.

It has been said, "Carry on with what you are doing." Why would anyone want to carry anything else on them? Isn't what you are already carrying enough on you in life?

*Casting all your care upon him; for he careth for you **(I Peter 5:7)***. *Come unto me, all ye that labour and are heavy laden, and I will give you rest. Take my yoke upon you, and learn of me; for I am meek and lowly in heart: and ye shall find rest unto your souls. For my yoke is easy, and my burden is light **(Matthew 11:28-30)***.

That which you don't see in the forecast, doesn't mean that it won't show up in the pourcast.

Weather Reporters announcements for the next three days.

The actual weather for the next three days.

Jesus is soon to come; He's the beat to our drum. That's the beat to our heart, and He will always be a part.

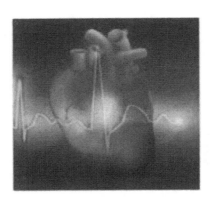

And then shall appear the sign of the Son of man in heaven: and then shall all the tribes of the earth mourn, and they shall see the Son of man coming in the clouds of heaven with power and great glory **(Matthew 24:30)**. *But of that day and hour knoweth no man, no, not the angels of heaven, but my Father only. But as the days of Noah were, so shall also the coming of the Son of man be. For as in the days that were before the flood they were eating and drinking, marrying and giving in marriage, until the day that Noe entered into the ark, And knew not until the flood came, and took them all away; so shall also the coming of the Son of man be* **(Matthew 24:36-39)**. *Speaking to yourselves in psalms and hymns and spiritual songs, singing and making melody in your heart to the Lord; Giving thanks always for all things unto God and the Father in the name of our Lord Jesus Christ;* **(Ephesians 5:19-20)**. *Always bearing about in the body the dying of the Lord Jesus, that the life also of Jesus might be made manifest in our body. For we which live are always delivered unto death for Jesus' sake, that the life also of Jesus might be made manifest in our mortal flesh* **(II Corinthians 4:10-11)**.

Jesus Christ is our ruler. That being said, the pains that He had suffered, we cannot measure up to.

*For even hereunto were ye called: because Christ also suffered for us, leaving us an example, that ye should follow his steps **(I Peter 2:21)**. Who hath measured the waters in the hollow of his hand, and meted out heaven with the span, and comprehended the dust of the earth in a measure, and weighed the mountains in scales, and the hills in a balance? Who hath directed the Spirit of the LORD, or being his counsellor hath taught him? With whom took he counsel, and who instructed*

him, and taught him in the path of judgment, and taught him knowledge, and shewed to him the way of understanding? Behold, the nations are as a drop of a bucket, and are counted as the small dust of the balance: behold, he taketh up the isles as a very little thing. And Lebanon is not sufficient to burn, nor the beasts thereof sufficient for a burnt offering. All nations before him are as nothing; and they are counted to him less than nothing, and vanity (Isaiah 40:12-17).

God is our guide and He gives us drive for our lives. It is He who takes us far, just like a car. He works like a four wheel drive, like His wheel/will for our lives, going in four directions, but He guides us in which path to go (North, South, East, or West). It is God who will guide your drive for life.

Shew me thy ways, O LORD; teach me thy paths. Lead me in thy truth, and teach me: for thou art the God of my salvation; on thee do I wait all the day (Psalms 25:4-5). Thou wilt shew me the path of life: in thy presence is fulness of joy; at thy right hand there are pleasures for evermore (Psalm 16:11). Hold up my goings in thy paths, that my footsteps slip not (Psalm 17:5). He restoreth my soul: he leadeth me in the paths of righteousness for his name's sake. Yea, though I walk through the valley of the shadow of death, I will fear no evil: for thou art with me; thy rod and thy staff they comfort me (Psalms 23:3-4).

In this society that we live in today, we make mistakes and some things are done intentional. Therefore, I ask, "Are things done by 'Accident' or 'Acts-I-dent'?"

> *Though he fall, he shall not be utterly cast down: for the LORD upholdeth him with his hand* ***(Psalm 37:24)***. *For if we sin wilfully after that we have received the knowledge of the truth, there remaineth no more sacrifice for sins* ***(Hebrews 10:26)***. *And have no fellowship with the unfruitful works of darkness, but rather reprove them* ***(Ephesians 5:11)***. *Therefore to him that knoweth to do good, and doeth it not, to him it is sin* ***(James 4:17)***. *How long will ye imagine mischief against a man? ye shall be slain all of you: as a bowing wall shall ye be, and as a tottering fence. They only consult to cast him down from his excellency: they delight in lies: they bless with their mouth, but they curse inwardly. Selah* ***(Psalms 62:3-4)***. *Fret not thyself because of evildoers, neither be thou envious against the workers of iniquity. For they shall soon be cut down like the grass, and wither as the green herb* ***(Psalms 37:1-2)***.

It's funny how people hate to be held up, but they love to be lifted up.

> *Rest in the LORD, and wait patiently for him: fret not thyself because of him who prospereth in his way, because of the man who bringeth wicked devices to pass* ***(Psalm 37:7)***.

The Lord's will is truth. Therefore, by His will/wheel we will drive for perfection to never miss a strike through His guidance. We will get a hit every time.

He is the Rock, his work is perfect: for all his ways are judgment: a God of truth and without iniquity, just and right is he **(Deuteronomy 32:4)**. *Trust in the* LORD *with all thine heart; and lean not unto thine own understanding. In all thy ways acknowledge him, and he shall direct thy paths* **(Proverbs 3:5-6)**. *And be not conformed to this world: but be ye transformed by the renewing of your mind, that ye may prove what is that good, and acceptable, and perfect, will of God* **(Romans 12:2)**. *Be ye therefore perfect, even as your Father which is in heaven is perfect* **(Matthew 5:48)**.

The Lord is our saviour, as He is our doctor. Do we go to the pulpit or to the pill pit to be healed? The pill pit is the container of medication that man prescribes. But, the pulpit is the altar that the Lord prescribes. The pulpit is the altar-meant (ultimate) power of healing that pulls you through salvation of God.

For thus saith the LORD, Thy bruise is incurable, and thy wound is grievous. There is none to plead thy cause, that thou mayest be bound up: thou hast no healing medicines

(Jeremiah 30:12-13). *And, behold, a woman, which was diseased with an issue of blood twelve years, came behind him, and touched the hem of his garment: For she said within herself, If I may but touch his garment, I shall be whole. But Jesus turned him about, and when he saw her, he said, Daughter, be of good comfort; thy faith hath made thee whole. And the woman was made whole from that hour (Matthew 9:20-22).*

"Afterward/After-word"

In many church services, there are cooks downstairs to prepare food for the congregation. The choir sings and the minister speaks on the word to eat of the fruit. Afterward/Afterword they eat food, and for dessert, they eat fruit.

He that hath an ear, let him hear what the Spirit saith unto the churches; To him that overcometh will I give to eat of the tree of life, which is in the midst of the paradise of God (Revelation 2:7). But his delight is in the law of the LORD; and in his law doth he meditate day and night. And he shall be like a tree planted by the rivers of water, that bringeth forth his fruit in his season; his leaf also shall not wither; and whatsoever he doeth shall prosper (Psalms 1:2-3). And having food and raiment let us be therewith content (I Timothy 6:8). For if I by grace be a partaker, why am I evil spoken of for that for which I give thanks? Whether therefore ye eat, or drink, or whatsoever ye do, do all to the glory of God (I Corinthians 10:30-31).

The Lord is about a move. It is depended on our don'ts and our do's/dues (tithes).

A heavenly move across/a cross the way.

*Likewise the Spirit also helpeth our infirmities: for we know not what we should pray for as we ought: but the Spirit itself maketh intercession for us with groanings which cannot be uttered. And he that searcheth the hearts knoweth what is the mind of the Spirit, because he maketh intercession for the saints according to the will of God. And we know that all things work together for good to them that love God, to them who are the called according to his purpose **(Romans 8:26-28)**. And that ye study to be quiet, and to do your own business, and to work with your own hands, as we commanded you; That ye may walk honestly toward them that are without, and that ye may have lack of nothing. **(I Thessalonians 4:11-12)**.*

Stars/Starrs are team players to enlighten the world, but Jesus is the "Most Valuable" All Star of all stars/starrs.

Then spake Jesus again unto them, saying, I am the light of the world: he that followeth me shall not walk in darkness, but shall have the light of life **(John 8:12)**.

The light is to the Son, as the sun is to the light.

And God said, Let there be light: and there was light **(Genesis 1:3)**. *Truly the light is sweet, and a pleasant thing it is for the eyes to behold the sun* **(Ecclesiastes 11:7)**. *The sun also ariseth, and the sun goeth down, and hasteth to his place where he arose* **(Ecclesiastes 1:5)**. *Then spake Jesus again unto them, saying, I am the light of the world: he that followeth me shall not walk in darkness, but shall have the light of life* **(John 8:12)**. *From the rising of the sun unto the going down of the same the* LORD*'s name is to be praised* **(Psalm 113:3)**.

God is our spiritual doctor, so we are His patients. Therefore, He wants us to be patient in His time of healing.

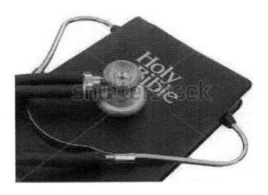

*And Jesus went about all Galilee, teaching in their synagogues, and preaching the gospel of the kingdom, and healing all manner of sickness and all manner of disease among the people. And his fame went throughout all Syria: and they brought unto him all sick people that were taken with divers diseases and torments, and those which were possessed with devils, and those which were lunatick, and those that had the palsy; and he healed them **(Matthew 4:23-24)**. Then shall thy light break forth as the morning, and thine health shall spring forth speedily: and thy righteousness shall go before thee; the glory of the LORD shall be thy reward **(Isaiah 58:8)**. But they that wait upon the LORD shall renew their strength; they shall mount up with wings as eagles; they shall run, and not be weary; and they shall walk, and not faint **(Isaiah 40:31)**.*

The Lord is looking for us to pray, and Satan is seeking whom he may devour for his prey.

The Lord looks for us to pray.   *Satan looks to us for his prey.*

Jesus answered and said unto them, Verily I say unto you, If ye have faith, and doubt not, ye shall not only do this which is done to the fig tree, but also if ye shall say unto this mountain, Be thou removed, and be thou cast into the sea; it shall be done. And all things, whatsoever ye shall ask in prayer, believing, ye shall receive **(Matthew 21:21-22)**. *And the prayer of faith shall save the sick, and the Lord shall raise him up; and if he have committed sins, they shall be forgiven him. Confess your faults one to another, and pray one for another, that ye may be healed. The effectual fervent prayer of a righteous man availeth much* **(James 5:15-16)**. *Be sober, be vigilant; because your adversary the devil, as a roaring lion, walketh about, seeking whom he may devour* **(I Peter 5:8)**. *I am weary of my crying: my throat is dried: mine eyes fail while I wait for my God* **(Psalm 69:3)**. *And kings shall be thy nursing fathers, and their queens thy nursing* *mothers: they shall bow down to thee with their face toward the earth, and lick up the dust of thy feet; and thou shalt know that I am the LORD: for they shall not be ashamed that wait for me* **(Isaiah 49:23)**. *Humble yourselves in the sight of the Lord, and he shall lift you up* **(James 4:10)**.

Let "Go" and let "God", but don't let go of God, because without God you have nowhere to "Go".

Cast thy burden upon the LORD, and he shall sustain thee: he shall never suffer the righteous to be moved **(Psalm 55:22)**. *Saying, Father, if thou be willing, remove this cup from me: nevertheless not my will, but thine, be done* **(Luke 22:42)**. *Whither shall I go from thy spirit? or whither shall I flee from thy presence? If I ascend up into heaven, thou art there: if I make my bed in hell, behold, thou art there. If I take the wings of the morning, and dwell in the uttermost parts of the sea; Even there shall thy hand lead me, and thy right hand shall hold me. If I say, Surely the darkness shall cover me; even the night shall be light about me. Yea, the darkness hideth not from thee; but the night shineth as the day: the darkness and the light are both alike to thee* **(Psalms 139:7-12)**.

Why is it that we are so excited to get in line to see a starr perform his/her act,

but we are slow to stand in line for God's act in our lives, who is the creator of all stars/starrs?

Thou shalt have no other gods before me. Thou shalt not make unto thee any graven image, or any likeness of any thing that is in heaven above, or that is in the earth beneath, or that is in the water under the earth. Thou shalt not bow down thyself to them, nor serve them: for I the LORD thy God am a jealous God, visiting the iniquity of the fathers upon the children unto the third and fourth generation of them that hate me (Exodus 20:3-5). For by him were all things created, that are in heaven, and that are in earth, visible and invisible, whether they be thrones, or dominions, or principalities, or powers: all things were created by him, and for him: And he is before all things, and by him all things consist (Colossians 1:16-17).

A person will say, "I am tired, and I need to get away from the rest (of the people)." But how can that be if Jesus is your rest? Aren't we supposed to be made in His image?

Come unto me, all ye that labour and are heavy laden, and I will give you rest. Take my yoke upon you, and learn of me; for I am meek and lowly in heart: and ye shall find rest unto your souls. For my yoke is easy, and my burden is light (Matthew 11:28-30). And God said, Let us make man in our image, after our likeness: and let them have dominion over the fish of the sea, and over the fowl of the air, and over the cattle, and over all the earth, and over every creeping thing that creepeth upon the earth (Genesis 1:26).

Here on earth, most houses have signs for an address, so you don't have to wonder and get lost. But, in God's house, there are many signs and wonders to be addressed so that you won't be lost.

*And these signs shall follow them that believe; In my name shall they cast out devils; they shall speak with new tongues; They shall take up serpents; and if they drink any deadly thing, it shall not hurt them; they shall lay hands on the sick, and they shall recover **(Mark 16:17-18)**. God also bearing them witness, both with signs and wonders, and with divers miracles, and gifts of the Holy Ghost, according to his own will **(Hebrews 2:4)**. The Lord is not slack concerning his promise, as some men count slackness; but is longsuffering to us-ward, not willing that any should perish, but that all should come to repentance **(II Peter 3:9)**. For this shall every one that is godly pray unto thee in a time when thou mayest be found: surely in the floods of great waters they shall not come nigh unto him **(Psalm 32:6)**. And be found in him, not having mine own righteousness, which is of the law, but that which is through the faith of Christ, the righteousness which is of God by faith **(Philippians 3:9)**. Wherefore, beloved, seeing that ye look for such things, be diligent that ye may be found of him in peace, without spot, and blameless **(II Peter 3:14)**.*

It is said that we are bound by strongholds from the past: Why not seek to be found and hold strong unto the Lord?

Instead of being bound by strongholds, hold on tight to God's word.

For though we walk in the flesh, we do not war after the flesh: (For the weapons of our warfare are not carnal, but mighty through God to the pulling down of strong holds) **(2 Corinthians 10:3-4)**. *For this my son was dead, and is alive again; he was lost, and is found. And they began to be merry* **(Luke 15:24)**. *Finally, my brethren, be strong in the Lord, and in the power of his might* **(Ephesians 6:10)**.

The Lord gives <u>upon us</u> blessings after blessings, but the Lord never gives <u>up on us</u>.

> *The blessing of the LORD, it maketh rich, and he addeth no sorrow with it* **(Proverbs 10:22)**. *And God is able to make all grace abound toward you; that ye, always having all sufficiency in all things, may abound to every good work: As it is written, HE HATH DISPERSED ABROAD; HE HATH GIVEN TO THE POOR: HIS RIGHTEOUSNESS REMAINETH FOR EVER* **(II Corinthians 9:8-9)**. *Blessings are upon the head of the just: but violence covereth the mouth of the wicked* **(Proverbs 10:6)**. *Let your conversation be without covetousness; and be content with such things as ye have: for he hath said, I WILL NEVER LEAVE THEE, NOR FORSAKE THEE* **(Hebrews 13:5)**.

So often, when we see or hear things that we don't want to deal with, we use the term "God forbid!" On the flipside, when we go through different trials and tribulations in life, we should Bid For God.

> *Trust in the LORD with all thine heart; and lean not unto thine own understanding. In all thy ways acknowledge him, and he shall direct thy paths. Be not wise in thine own eyes: fear the LORD, and depart from evil. It shall be health to thy navel, and marrow to thy bones* **(Proverbs 3:5-8)**. *These things I have spoken unto you, that in me ye might have peace. In the world ye shall have tribulation: but be of good cheer; I have overcome the world* **(John 16:33)**.

It's something how we can see-son Jesus, when we need more power, and we can also season (sea-son) in God's word to marinade in His power.

> *And then shall they see the Son of man coming in a cloud with power and great glory* **(Luke 21:27)**. *Behold, I give unto you power to tread on serpents and scorpions, and over all the power of the enemy: and nothing shall by any means hurt you* **(Luke 10:19)**. *But his delight is in the law of the LORD; and in his law doth he meditate day and night. And he shall be like a tree planted by the rivers of water, that bringeth forth his fruit in his season; his leaf also shall not wither; and whatsoever he doeth shall prosper* **(Psalms 1:2-3)**. *Let me understand the teaching of your precepts; then I will meditate on your wonders* **(Psalm 119:27)**.

Words from the wise is to enhance one's mind. On the flip side, words form the wise to enhance his/her mind.

> *Who hath put wisdom in the inward parts? or who hath given understanding to the heart* **(Job 38:36)**? *But where shall wisdom be found? and where is the place of understanding? Man knoweth not the price thereof; neither is it found in the land of the living. The depth saith, It is not in me: and the sea saith, It is not with me. It cannot be gotten for gold, neither shall silver be weighed for the price thereof. It cannot be valued*

with the gold of Ophir, with the precious onyx, or the sapphire. The gold and the crystal cannot equal it: and the exchange of it shall not be for jewels of fine gold. No mention shall be made of coral, or of pearls: for the price of wisdom is above rubies **(Job 28:12-18)**. *Wisdom is the principal thing; therefore get wisdom: and with all thy getting get understanding* **(Proverbs 4:7)**.

You may take chances in life by making a U-turn, as you are driving behind your own wheel/will in a car. Chances are, you will be ticketed where a fee is involved. If you make an S-turn, you will let Satan be your guide. His wheel/will is to take you down a zigzag road, which is the road of confusion. If you stay behind his wheel/will, you will slip, and fall off the cliff, because Satan comes to kill, steal, and destroy. You will pay for more than a ticket; you will pay with your life. Therefore, let Jesus be your guide, whose ticket is for free, and He will guide you with a "J-turn" in His direction.

If any man will do his will, he shall know of the doctrine, whether it be of God, or whether I speak of myself **(John 7:17)**. *The thief cometh not, but for to steal, and to kill, and to destroy: I am come that they might have life, and that they might have it more abundantly* **(John 10:10)**. *Howbeit when he, the Spirit of truth, is come, he will guide you into all truth: for he shall not speak of himself; but whatsoever he shall hear, that shall he speak: and he will shew you things to come* **(John 16:13)**.

A devastation is a derivative from the devil's station.

> *For we wrestle not against flesh and blood, but against principalities, against powers, against the rulers of the darkness of this world, against spiritual wickedness in high places (**Ephesians 6:12**). Even him, whose coming is after the working of Satan with all power and signs and lying wonders, And with all deceivableness of unrighteousness in them that perish; because they received not the love of the truth, that they might be saved. And for this cause God shall send them strong delusion, that they should believe a lie: That they all might be damned who believed not the truth, but had pleasure in unrighteousness (**2 Thessalonians 2:9-12**).*

It is said, "Taste and see that the Lord is good." He is seasoned all year around.

> *How sweet are thy words unto my taste! yea, sweeter than honey to my mouth (**Psalm 119:103**).*

If you stick with God's <u>consent</u>, then you will be <u>sent</u> by God. On the contrary, if you are sent by God, then you won't be <u>con</u>ned by man.

> *Let as many servants as are under the yoke count their own masters worthy of all honour, that the name of God and his doctrine be not blasphemed. And they that have believing masters, let them not despise them, because they are brethren; but rather do them service, because they are faithful and beloved, partakers of the benefit. These things teach and exhort. If any man teach otherwise, and consent not to wholesome words, even the words of our Lord Jesus Christ, and to the doctrine which is according to godliness; He is proud, knowing nothing, but doting about questions and strifes of words, whereof cometh envy, strife, railings, evil surmisings, Perverse disputings of men of corrupt minds, and destitute of the truth, supposing that gain is godliness: from such withdraw thyself. But godliness with contentment is great gain (**I Timothy 6:1-6**).*

Don't marry a person by the way they walk, but your walk with God makes your relationship merry.

> *A merry heart maketh a cheerful countenance: but by sorrow of the heart the spirit is broken (**Proverbs 15:13**). There is therefore now no condemnation to them which are in Christ Jesus, who walk not after the flesh, but after the spirit (**Romans 8:1**).*

151

If you do not write your plans, through God's will with a pen, will not the devil have you pinned through his plans and rights/writes? On the contrary, a pencil can be erased, so why give the devil access and place to your life, to be erased of your rights/writes through God's plans?

Where there is no vision, the people perish: but he that keepeth the law, happy is he **(Proverbs 29:18)**. *And the Lord answered me, and said, Write the vision, and make it plain upon tables, that he may run that readeth it. For the vision is yet for an appointed time, but at the end it shall speak, and not lie: though it tarry, wait for it; because it will surely come, it will not tarry* **(Habakkuk 2:2-3)**. *A man's heart deviseth his way: but the LORD directeth his steps* **(Proverbs 16:9)**. *Commit thy works unto the LORD, and thy thoughts shall be established* **(Proverbs 16:3)**.

Jesus' <u>fact</u>ory never starts slacking. Moreover, His <u>fact </u>will never slack.

The Lord is not slack concerning his promise, as some men count slackness; but is longsuffering to usward, not willing that any should perish, but that all should come to repentance **(2 Peter 3:9)**.

When you have a suit in court, shall you be suited for the judge, or should you come as you are for the suit against you, or the suit that you are in?

Both parties in house shall be tied up from the start, as the judge takes no sides. It supposed to be a clear sharp cut down the middle of the suit.

Why should the judge take suit on one side because of what you add-dress to your being an in/vest (investment)?

Is a suit that is a three piece better than a two piece,

Three Piece Suit   *Two Piece Suit*

or is the judge a/fraud (afraid) and opinionize to penalize/pen-a-lie, or pin-a-tie for one body over the other? There is a saying, "You can't judge a book by its cover." Well, a judge should not judge a body by its looks in a suit, but work over facts and not acts. It has also been said that a judge shall keep a track record of criminals. With that being said, if judges are supposed to have track records, then whom are they to judge? Isn't God our only judge that resides in heaven? Once again, when we go to God's house should we be suited, and act our best, or come as we are?

> *But why dost thou judge thy brothter? or why dost thou set at nought thy brother? for we shall all stand before the judgement seat of Christ. For it is written, AS I LIVE SAITH THE LORD, EVERY KNEE SHALL BOW TO ME, AND EVERY TONGUE SHALL CONFESS TO GOD. So then every one of us shall give account of himself to God **(Romans 14:10-12)**. Judge not, that ye be not judged. For with what judgment ye judge, ye shall be judged: and with what measure ye mete, it shall be measured to you again. And why beholdest thou the mote that is in thy brother's eye, but considerest not the beam that is in thine own eye? Or how wilt thou say to thy brother, Let me pull out the mote out of thine eye; and, behold, a beam is in thine own eye? Thou hypocrite, first cast out the beam out of thine own eye; and then shalt see clearly to cast out the mote out of thy brother's eye* **(Matthew 7:1-5)**. *For there is no respect of persons with God* **(Romans 2:11)**.

When you walk the concrete about the grounds of the earth, and the concrete is as the coals of fire, does not God give us the power to walk as Kings and Queens over the cold/coal remarks of the devil, in faith, to give him more heat? As we walk over the cold remarks of the devil, that will only melt the ice, and increase the heat on his flames.

> *For thou shalt heap coals of fire upon his head, and the Lord shall reward thee **(Proverbs 25:22)**. Therefore if thine enemy hunger, feed him; if he thirst, give him drink: for in so doing thou shalt heap coals of fire on his head **(Romans 12:20)**. Behold, I give unto you power to tread on serpents and scorpions, and over all the power of the enemy: and nothing shall by any means hurt you **(Luke 10:19)**.*

When the Lord reigns on us, He wants our spirit to grow as flowers from a feel/field of light.

> *For ALL FLESH IS AS GRASS, AND ALL THE GLORY OF MAN AS THE FLOWER OF GRASS. THE GRASS WITHERETH, AND THE FLOWERTHEREOF FALLETH AWAY **(1 Peter 1:24-25)**: The voice said, Cry. And he said, What shall I cry? All flesh is grass, and all goodliness thereof is as the flower of the field: The grass withereth, the flower fadeth: because the spirit of the LORD bloweth upon it: surely the people is grass **(Isaiah 40:6-7)**. Let the field be joyful, and all that is*

*therein: then shall all the trees of the wood rejoice **(Psalm 96:12)**. And hast made us unto our God kings and priests: and we shall reign on the earth **(Revelation 5:10)**.*

If we build up trust over time, shouldn't we trust in God who is <u>over time </u>and works <u>overtime </u>(OT)?

*Behold ye among the heathen, and regard, and wonder marvelously: for I will work a work in your days, which ye will not believe, though it be told you **(Habakkuk 1:5)**. And he said unto them, It is not for you to know the time or the seasons, which the Father hath put in his own power **(Acts 1:7)**. I must work the works of him that sent me, while it is day: the night cometh, who no man can work. As long as I am in the world, I am the light of the world **(John 9:4-5)**. Now unto him that is able to do exceeding abundantly about all that we ask or think, according to the power that worketh in us, unto him be glory in the church by Christ Jesus throughout all ages, world without end. A-men' **(Ephesians 3:20-21)**.*

"Traffic Directors"

If a human was a red light we would be in a world of trouble, but by Jesus' blood we are saved/safe. Aren't there enough humans that act naught/not of God who acts of this world, that can take up for every red light. On the other hand, Moses parted the Red Sea for the children of Israel to go through for everyone to see, and that "Is-Real".

*God is our refuge and strength, a very present help in trouble. Therefore will not we fear, though the earth be removed, and though the mountains be carried into the midst of the sea; Though the waters thereof roar and be troubled, though the mountain shake with the swelling thereof. Selah **(Psalms 46:1-3)**. And Moses said unto the people, Fear ye not, stand still, and see the salvation of the LORD, which he will shew to you to day: for the Egyptians whom ye have seen to day, ye shall see them again no more for ever. The LORD shall fight for you, and ye shall hold your peace. And the LORD said unto Moses, Wherefore criest thou unto me? speak unto the children of Israel, that they go forward But lift thou up thy rod, and stretch out thine hand over the sea, and divide it: and the children of Israel shall go on dry ground through the midst of the sea **(Exodus 14:13-16)**.*

We should not do evil for evil. That will only bring about more evil. But, if someone does evil onto you, turn it around to live. That comes through fasting and praying.

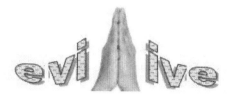

Moreover, if you turn "bʌd" around for "bʌd", it will still be "bʌd".

 turned around is still

That goes back to: negative (-) X negative (-), through Christ Jesus, does not turn things around for a positive.

Finally, be ye all of one mind, having compassion one of another, love as brethren, be pitiful, be courteous: Not rending evil for evil, or railing for railing: but contrariwise blessing; knowing that ye are thereunto called, that ye should inherit a blessing. For HE THAT WILL LOVE LIFE, AND SEE GOOD DAYS, LET HIM REFRAIN HIS TONGUE FROM EVIL, AND HIS LIPS THAT THEY SPEAK NO GUILE: LET HIM ESCHEW EVIL, AND DO GOOD; LET HIM SEEK PEACE, AND ENSUE IT. FOR THE EYES OF THE LORD ARE OVER THE RIGHTOUS, AND HIS EARS ARE OPEN UNTO THEIR PRAYERS: BUT THE FACE OF THE LORD IS AGAINST THEM THAT DO EVIL (1 Peter 3:8-12).

When you get frustrated/<u>fuss</u>-ta-<u>rated</u>, does not your temperature rise, and get <u>curse</u>-ta-<u>rated</u>/cursed-or-rated?

When Adam listened to Eve (his wife), regarding the eating of the fruit, did they rise? On the contrary, when the grounds were cursed, were not Adam and Eve also grounded by God?

And unto Adam he said, Because thou hast hearkened unto the voice of thy wife, and hast eaten of the tree, of which I commanded thee, saying, thou shalt not eat of it: cursed is the ground for thy sake; in sorrow shalt thou eat of it all the days of thy life; Thorns also and thistles shall it bring forth to thee; and thou shalt eat the herb of the field; in the sweat of thy face shalt thou eat bread, till thou return unto the ground; for out of it wast thou taken: for dust thou art, and unto dust shalt thou return **(Genesis 3:17-19)**

O my soul, come not thou into their secret; unto their assembly, mine honour, be not thou united: for in their anger they slew a man, and in their selfwill they digged down a wall **(Genesis 49:6)**. *Blessed is the man that walketh not in the counsel of the ungodly, nor standeth in the way of sinners, nor sitteth in the seat of the scornful. But his delight is in the law of the LORD; and in his law doth he meditate day and night* **(Psalms 1:1-2)**. *Thus saith the LORD; Cursed be the man that trusteth in man, and maketh flesh his arm, and whose heart departeth from the LORD* **(Jeremiah 17:5)**. *A soft answer turneth away wrath: but grievous words stir up anger. The tongue of the wise useth knowledge aright: but the mouth of fools poureth out foolishness* **(Proverbs 15:1)**. *Stand in awe, and sin not: commune with your own heart upon your bed, and be still. Selah. Offer the sacrifices of righteousness, and put your trust in the LORD* **(Psalms 4:4-5)**.

The Lord left/lift us to be equipped in the spirit. Therefore, we should not quit on Him, because He will never leave us.

> *Blessed be the Lord my strength which teacheth my hands to war, and my fingers to fight: My goodness, and my fortress; my high tower, and my deliverer; my shield, and he in whom I trust; who subdueth my people under me* **(Psalms 144:1-2)**. *All scripture is given by inspiration of God, and is profitable for doctrine, for reproof, for correction, for instruction in righteousness: That the man of God may be perfect, thoroughly furnished unto all good works* **(2 Timothy 3:16-17)**. *Let your conversation be without covetousness; and be content with such things as ye have: for he hath said, I will never leave thee, nor forsake thee. So that we may boldly say, The Lord is my helper, and I will not fear what man shall do unto me* **(Hebrews 13:5-6)**.

Isn't it something how a person with a disability is treated unfair, or wrong? Just because a person has a disability does not give any other person the ability to dis.

> *Therefore all things whatsoever ye would that men should do to you, do ye even so to them: for this is the law and the prophets* **(Matthew 7:12)**.

161

When we are born again as children of God, we will come out of the water <u>RAW</u>, just like rinsing food (in water) before heating it. But, as we become stronger in Christ, He will turn us around for <u>WAR</u>. After being rinsed in baptism, shouldn't we be heated for the Lord, as we become stronger in Christ?

 turning around for

*Then Peter said unto them, Repent, and be baptized every one of you in the name of Jesus Christ for the remission of sins, and ye shall receive the gift of the Holy Ghost **(Acts 2:38)**. Being born again, not of corruptible seed, but of incorruptible, by the word of God, which liveth and abideth for ever **(1 Peter 1:23)**. The like figure whereunto even baptism doth also now save us (not the putting away of the filth of the flesh, but the answer of a good conscience toward God,) by the resurrection of Jesus Christ **(1 Peter 3:21)**: God is my strength and power: and he maketh my way perfect. He maketh my feet like hinds' feet: and setteth me upon my high places. He teacheth my hands to war; so that a bow of steel is broken by mine arms. Thou hast also given me the shield of thy salvation: and thy gentleness hath made me great. Thou hast enlarged my steps under me; so that my feet did not slip. I have pursued mine enemies, and destroyed them; and turned not again until I had consumed them. And*

*I have consumed them, and wounded them, that they could not arise: yea, they are fallen under my feet. For thou hast girded me with strength to battle: them that rose up against me hast thou subdued under me **(2 Samuel 22:33-40)**. Blessed be the LORD my strength which teacheth my hands to war, and my fingers to fight: My goodness, and my fortress; my high tower, and my deliverer; my shield, and he in whom I trust; who subdueth my people under me **(Psalms 144:1-2)**.*

The Lord's band-stations are requirements/choir-ments for His manifestation.

*Make a joy noise unto the LORD, all ye lands. Serve the Lord with gladness: come before his presence with singing **(Psalms 100:1-2)**.*

When you listen and receive from the Lord, He will give you a keen/king's mind.

*A wise man will hear, and will increase learning; and a man of understanding shall attain unto wise counsels **(Proverbs 1:5)**:*

163

Take the speck out of your own eye before you take the speck out of someone else's eye if you want respect through the eyes of another person. If you have not removed the speck from your own eye, how can you x-speck/expect removement from your brother's eye. Can you see what you are doing, or do you go plank/blank through your own faults/false? You may turn out to be nosey/no-see.

lank

lank

As "Blank" is to "Plank", and "Plank" is to Zero (0), where they are both equal to each other, doesn't nothing from nothing equal nothing? Therefore, How will you be able to see another person's mistake if you can't see your own, or are you just nosey/no-see?

When you pull the mote out of your eye, then you will be re-mote to see your brother's eye, and perhaps, be an eyewitness to him.

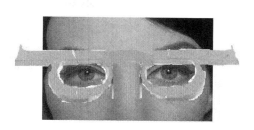

When you correct your vision, then you can
see to help your brother's.

New King James Version (NKJV)

*And why do you look at the speck in your
brother's eye, but do not consider the plank in
your own eye? Or how can you say to your
brother, 'Let me remove the speck from your eye';
and look, a plank is in your own eye? Hypocrite!
First remove the plank from your own eye, and
then you will see clearly to remove the speck from
your brother's eye* **(Matthew 7:3-5)**.

King James Version (KJV)

*And why beholdest thou the mote that is in thy
brother's eye, but considerest not the beam that is
in thine own eye? Or how wilt thou say to thy
brother, Let me pull out the mote out of thine eye;
and, behold, a beam is in thine own eye? Thou
hypocrite, first cast out the beam out of thine own
eye; and then shalt thou see clearly to cast out the
mote out of thy brother's eye* **(Matthew 7:3-5)**.

That which was from the beginning, which we have heard, which we have seen with our eyes, which we have looked upon, and our hands have handled, of the Word of life; (For the life was manifested, and we have seen it, and bear witness, and shew unto you that eternal life, which was with the Father, and was manifested unto us;) That which we have seen and heard declare we unto you, that ye also may have fellowship with us: and truly our fellowship is with the Father, and with his Son Jesus Christ **(1 John 1:1-3)**.

It's something how we can flip a coin for heads or tails, for our faith and belief of what we may desire in life (on earth). Why not have belief and faith by flipping through God's word, that has no tales, but He tells us the truth? His word will also make us head over all nations.

All scripture is given by inspiration of God, and is profitable for doctrine, for reproof, for correction, for instruction in righteousness **(2 Timothy 3:16)**: *Get wisdom, get understanding: forget [it] not; neither decline from the words of my mouth* **(Proverbs 4:5)**. *And be not conformed to this world: but be ye transformed by the renewing of your mind, that ye may prove what is that good, and acceptable, and perfect, will of God* **(Romans 12:2)**. *And the LORD shall make thee the head, and not the tail; and thou shalt be above only, and thou shalt not be beneath; if that thou*

166

*hearken unto the commandments of the LORD thy God, which I command thee this day, to observe and to do them **(Deuteronomy 28:13)**: Study to shew thyself approved unto God, a workman that needeth not to be ashamed, rightly dividing the word of truth **(2 Timothy 2:15)**. And the world passeth away, and the lust thereof: but he that doeth the will of God abideth for ever **(1 John 2:17)**.*

A drawer of Christ on the flip side, is reward.

"REWARD" is "DRAWER" spelled backward.

*And in that day thou shalt say, O Lord, I will praise thee: though thou wast angry with me, thine anger is turned away, and thou comfortedst me. Behold, God is my salvation; I will trust, and not be afraid: for the Lord Jehovah is my strength and my song; he also is become my salvation. Therefore with joy shall ye draw water out of the wells of salvation. And in that day shall ye say, Praise the Lord, call upon his name, declare his doings among the people, make mention that his name is exalted **(Isaiah 12:1-4)**.*

At One time I worked for this company "Iron Fountain". I gave them a <u>pizza</u>-my-mind, after they released me of my duties, and I made them take heed/eat. I gave them:

> ➢ **Uppercuts**

> ➢ **Side-cuts**

> ➢ **And Jabs**

with a punch (drink) in their mouth.

It was a knock out party for them. All they could do is roll over from hurt. They grounded me, and I grounded them back with punch-ure (puncture). The only difference is, I did it by delivering to them love and kindness. The Lord blessed me to reach a high degree of excellence in Him. Isn't it something how the Lord can move mountains in the midst of your troubles? *(True Story)*

*But I say unto you, Love your enemies, bless them that curse you, do good to them that hate you, and pray for them which despitefully use you, and persecute you **(Matthew 5:44)**; Therefore IF THINE ENEMY HUNGER, FEED HIM; IF HE THRIST, GIVE HIM DRINK: FOR IN SO DOING THOU SHALT HEAP COALS OF FIRE ON HIS HEAD. Be not overcome of evil, but overcome evil with good **(Romans 12:20-21)**. When a man's ways please the LORD, he maketh even his enemies to be at peace with him **(Proverbs 16:7)**.*

The Lord is an artist above all artists. He will draw you closer if you let Him. Doesn't He art in heaven?

> And I, if I be lifted up from the earth, will draw all men unto me *(John 12:32)*. And he said unto them, When ye pray, say, Our Father which art in heaven, Hallowed be thy name. Thy kingdom come. Thy will be done, as in heaven, so in earth *(Luke 11:2)*.

CHAPTER 3

ANALOGIES

If you give God praise for a half full cup,
He will bless you with doors that won't shut.

Half full cup vs *Door that won't shut*

*Thou preparest a table before me in the presence of mine enemies: thou anointest my head with oil; my cup runneth over **(Psalm 23:5)**.*

Now-a-days, people are so uptight, and they don't act right. We as a whole will do better if we allow Jesus Christ to instruct our walk in life.

*A new heart also will I give you, and a new spirit will I put within you: and I will take away the stony heart out of your flesh, and I **(Ezekiel 36:26)**. I will instruct thee and teach thee in the way which thou shalt go: I will guide thee with mine eye **(Psalm 32:8)**.*

God had made woman from a rib of a man, and it was all due to His plan. The man's name was Adam, and the woman's name was Eve. They were brought together as one, as both were meant to cleave.

> *Therefore the LORD God sent him forth from the garden of Eden, to till the ground from whence he was taken. So he drove out the man; and he placed at the east of the garden of Eden Cher'-u-bims, and a flaming sword which turned every way, to keep the way of the tree of life* **(Genesis 3:23-24)**.

The Lord is the answer to our everyday life, and it is Satan who causes strife.

> *For God is not the author of confusion, but of peace, as in all churches of the saints* **(I Corinthians 14:33)**. *The sacrifice of the wicked is an abomination to the LORD: but the prayer of the upright is his delight* **(Proverbs 15:8)**.

Keep a smile on your face and never let it go to waste.

> *A merry heart maketh a cheerful countenance: but by sorrow of the heart the spirit is broken* **(Proverbs 15:13)**.

Stay in prayer and know God care.

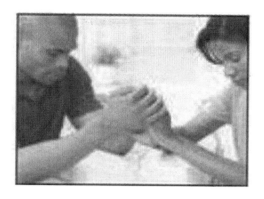

Pray without ceasing. In every thing give thanks: for this is the will of God in Christ Jesus concerning you **(I Thessalonians 5:17-18)**. *Rejoicing in hope; patient in tribulation; continuing instant in prayer* **(Romans 12:12)**.

When Satan gives you advice it won't be nice, and when the Lord gives you advice, its value can't hold a price.

Whoso loveth instruction loveth knowledge: but he that hateth reproof is brutish. A good man obtaineth favour of the LORD: but a man of wicked devices will he condemn **(Proverbs 12:1-2)**. *Apply thine heart unto instruction, and thine ears to the words of knowledge* **(Proverbs 23:12)**.

You have to be consistent in praying when you're up and when you're down. You also have to be repetitious in praying when you're happy and when you frown.

> *Give ear to my words, O LORD, consider my meditation. Hearken unto the voice of my cry, my King, and my God: for unto thee will I pray* **(Psalms 5:1-2)**. *Cast thy burden upon the* LORD, *and he shall sustain thee: he shall never suffer the righteous to be moved* **(Psalm 55:22)**.

When you stay quiet and humble, you don't stumble, in someone else's fumble.

> *Humble yourselves therefore under the mighty hand of God, that he may exalt you in due time: Casting all your care upon him; for he careth for you* **(I Peter 5:6-7)**. *And that ye study to be quiet, and to do your own business, and to work with your own hands, as we commanded you; That ye may walk honestly toward them that are without, and that ye may have lack of nothing* **(I Thessalonians 4:11-12)**.

When things in life go wrong, they won't last for long.

> *For which cause we faint not; but though our outward man perish, yet the inward man is renewed day by day. For our light affliction, which is but for a moment, worketh for us a far more exceeding and eternal weight of glory; While we look not at the things which are seen, but at the things which are not seen: for the things which are seen are temporal; but the things which are not seen are eternal* **(II Corinthians 4:16-18)**. *And we know that all things work together for good to them that love God, to them who are the called according to his purpose. For whom he did foreknow, he also did predestinate to be conformed to the image of his Son, that he might be the firstborn among many brethren. Moreover whom he did predestinate, them he also called: and whom he called, them he also justified: and whom he justified, them he also glorified. What shall we then say to these things? If God be for us, who can be against us* **(Romans 8:28-31)**?

When the Lord enlarges your territory that will enhance your testimonial story.

> *We are fools for Christ's sake, but ye are wise in Christ; we are weak, but ye are strong; ye are honourable, but we are despised* **(I Corinthians 4:10)**.

The highest praise is "Hallelujah" and don't let nobody out do yah.

Praise ye the LORD. Sing unto the LORD a new song, and his praise in the congregation of saints **(Psalm 149:1)**. *And after these things I heard a great voice of much people in heaven, saying, Alleluia; Salvation, and glory, and honour, and power, unto the Lord our God* **(Revelation 19:1)**.

Comfort for the depressed, when you go through, it's only a test.

These things I have spoken unto you, that in me ye might have peace. In the world ye shall have tribulation: but be of good cheer; I have overcome the world **(John 16:33)**. *And not only so, but we glory in tribulations also: knowing that tribulation worketh patience* **(Romans 5:3)**. *Rejoicing in hope; patient in tribulation; continuing instant in prayer* **(Romans 12:12)**.

The Lord wants us to meditate in His book, to learn and do of His ways so we won't be cooked.

*Study to shew thyself approved unto God, a workman that needeth not to be ashamed, rightly dividing the word of truth **(II Timothy 2:15)**. But his delight is in the law of the LORD; and in his law doth he meditate day and night. And he shall be like a tree planted by the rivers of water, that bringeth forth his fruit in his season; his leaf also shall not wither; and whatsoever he doeth shall prosper **(Psalms 1:2-3)**. But the fearful, and unbelieving, and the abominable, and murderers, and whoremongers, and sorcerers, and idolaters, and all liars, shall have their part in the lake which burneth with fire and brimstone: which is the second death **(Revelation 21:8)**.*

The Lord wants us in His word as a fruit or get the boot, and to not act cute.

*Blessed is the man that walketh not in the counsel of the ungodly, nor standeth in the way of sinners, nor sitteth in the seat of the scornful. But his delight is in the law of the LORD; and in his law doth he meditate day and night. And he shall be like a tree planted by the rivers of water, that bringeth forth his fruit in his season; his leaf also shall not wither; and whatsoever he doeth shall prosper **(Psalms 1:1-3)**.*

God's got a blessing with your name on it. Give God praise in knowing there is no shame on it.

And ye shall eat in plenty, and be satisfied, and praise the name of the LORD your God, that hath dealt wondrously with you: and my people shall never be ashamed **(Joel 2:26)**. *And I will make them and the places round about my hill a blessing; and I will cause the shower to come down in his season; there shall be showers of blessing* **(Ezekiel 34:26)**.

Give your hands a raise, and give God the praise.

Thus will I bless thee while I live: I will lift up my hands in thy name. My soul shall be satisfied as with marrow and fatness; and my mouth shall praise thee with joyful lips **(Psalms 63:4-5)**.

When you invest with the best you'll be blessed.

> *Bring ye all the tithes into the storehouse, that there may be meat in mine house, and prove me now herewith, saith the LORD of hosts, if I will not open you the windows of heaven, and pour you out a blessing, that there shall not be room enough to receive it* **(Malachi 3:10)**.

If you don't let it go, your worries will build up and show.

> *Cast thy burden upon the LORD, and he shall sustain thee: he shall never suffer the righteous to be moved* **(Psalm 55:22)**. *Heaviness in the heart of man maketh it stoop: but a good word maketh it glad* **(Proverbs 12:25)**.

If God leads you through life, then He won't leave you with strife.

> *I will instruct thee and teach thee in the way which thou shalt go: I will guide thee with mine eye* **(Psalm 32:8)**. *A wrathful man stirreth up strife: but he that is slow to anger appeaseth strife* **(Proverbs 15:18)**. *Only by pride cometh contention: but with the well advised is wisdom* **(Proverbs 13:10)**.

God is a jealous God, and He's also a restless God.

*Thou shalt not bow down thyself to them, nor serve them: for I the LORD thy God am a jealous God, visiting the iniquity of the fathers upon the children unto the third and fourth generation of them that hate me **(Exodus 20:5)**. I will lift up mine eyes unto the hills, from whence cometh my help. My help cometh from the LORD, which made heaven and earth. He will not suffer thy foot to be moved: he that keepeth thee will not slumber. Behold, he that keepeth Israel shall neither slumber nor sleep **(Psalms 121:1-4)**.*

The more that you are truthful, and praise the Lord, the more in Heaven will be your reward.

*And, behold, I come quickly; and my reward is with me, to give every man according as his work shall be **(Revelation 22:12)**. Blessed is the man that endureth temptation: for when he is tried, he shall receive the crown of life, which the Lord hath promised to them that love him **(James 1:12)**. Rejoice ye in that day, and leap for joy: for, behold, your reward is great in heaven: for in the like manner did their fathers unto the prophets **(Luke 6:23)**.*

A go getter's not a quitter.

*And Jesus answering saith unto them, Have faith in God. For verily I say unto you, That whosoever shall say unto this mountain, Be thou removed, and be thou cast into the sea; and shall not doubt in his heart, but shall believe that those things which he saith shall come to pass; he shall have whatsoever he saith. Therefore I say unto you, What things soever ye desire, when ye pray, believe that ye receive them, and ye shall have them **(Mark 11:22-24)**.*

You have to speak bold against strongholds.

*For the weapons of our warfare are not carnal, but mighty through God to the pulling down of strong holds **(II Corinthians 10:4)**.*

My blessings may be delayed, but not betrayed.

> *Wait on the LORD: be of good courage, and he shall strengthen thine heart: wait, I say, on the LORD (Psalm 27:14). My brethren, count it all joy when ye fall into divers temptations; Knowing this, that the trying of your faith worketh patience. But let patience have her perfect work, that ye may be perfect and entire, wanting nothing (James 1:2-4).*

We all have to know that a change is going to come. To the sweet music of the Holy Spirit, play a tune with your hum.

> *Speaking to yourselves in psalms and hymns and spiritual songs, singing and making melody in your heart to the Lord; Giving thanks always for all things unto God and the Father in the name of our Lord Jesus Christ (Ephesians 5:19-20). Be careful for nothing; but in every thing by prayer and supplication with thanksgiving let your requests be made known unto God. And the peace of God, which passeth all understanding, shall keep your hearts and minds through Christ Jesus (Philippians 4:6-7).*

We have to be patient in the days that we wait, because God doesn't operate by date, but our days are operated by Him.

With God, there's no dates allowed.

For my thoughts are not your thoughts, neither are your ways my ways, saith the LORD. For as the heavens are higher than the earth, so are my ways higher than your ways, and my thoughts than your thoughts **(Isaiah 55:8-9)**. *But if we hope for that we see not, then do we with patience wait for it* **(Romans 8:25)**. *But, beloved, be not ignorant of this one thing, that one day is with the Lord as a thousand years, and a thousand years as one day. The Lord is not slack concerning His promise, as Some men count slackness; but is longsuffering to usward, not willing that any should perish, but that all should come to repentance* **(II Peter 3:8-9)**.

Have faith; don't feel blue, because God, our Father, is going to bless you.

*Be not deceived; God is not mocked: for whatsoever a man soweth, that shall he also reap. For he that soweth to his flesh shall of the flesh reap corruption; but he that soweth to the Spirit shall of the Spirit reap life everlasting. And let us not be weary in well doing: for in due season we shall reap, if we faint not. As we have therefore opportunity, let us do good unto all men, especially unto them who are of the household of faith **(Galatians 6:7-10)**. But without faith it is impossible to please him: for he that cometh to God must believe that he is, and that he is a rewarder of them that diligently seek him **(Hebrews 11:6)**.*

God gave us lips to quote His scripts.

*As newborn babes, desire the sincere milk of the word, that ye may grow thereby: If so be ye have tasted that the Lord is gracious **(I Peter 2:2-3)**. But when they deliver you up, take no thought how or what ye shall speak: for it shall be given you in that same hour what ye shall speak. For it is not ye that speak, but the Spirit of your Father which speaketh in you **(Matthew 10:19-20)**.*

Do a Holy Ghost dance on the devil, and stomp him to a deeper level.

Let them praise his name in the dance: let them sing praises unto him with the timbrel and harp **(Psalm 149:3)**. *Behold, I give unto you power to tread on serpents and scorpions, and over all the power of the enemy: and nothing shall by any means hurt you* **(Luke 10:19)**.

There's 365 days in a year to give our Lord some cheer.

The days of our years are threescore years and ten; and if by reason of strength they be fourscore years, yet is their strength labour and sorrow; for it is soon cut off, and we fly away **(Psalm 90:10)**. *I will bless the LORD at all times: his praise shall continually be in my mouth. My soul shall make her boast in the LORD: the humble shall hear thereof, and be glad. O magnify the LORD with me, and let us exalt his name together* **(Psalms 34:1-3)**.

Do a Holy Ghost dance and don't give the devil a chance.

Let them praise his name in the dance: let them sing praises unto him with the timbrel and harp. For the LORD taketh pleasure in his people: he will beautify the meek with salvation **(Psalms 149:3-4)**.

Eating too much of the wrong foods can add on pounds, and add on of pounds can give one frowns.

For he that eateth and drinketh unworthily, eateth and drinketh damnation to himself, not discerning the Lord's body **(I Corinthians 11:29)**. *But put ye on the Lord Jesus Christ, and make not provision for the flesh, to fulfil the lusts thereof* **(Romans 13:14)**.

The Lord is due a praise shabach and don't let it stop.

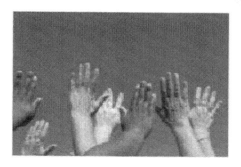

I will extol thee, my God, O king; and I will bless thy name for ever and ever. Every day will I bless thee; and I will praise thy name for ever and ever. Great is the LORD, and greatly to be praised; and his greatness is unsearchable **(Psalms 145:1-3)**.

Expect greatness, and knowing God, there's no lateness.

He hath made every thing beautiful in his time: also he hath set the world in their heart, so that no man can find out the work that God maketh from the beginning to the end **(Ecclesiastes 3:11)**. *For if the word spoken by angels was stedfast, and every transgression and disobedience received a just recompence of reward; How shall we escape, if we neglect so great salvation; which at the first began to be spoken by the Lord, and was confirmed unto us by them that heard him;* **(Hebrews 2:2-3)**.

Lift up holy hands, and don't give Satan a chance.

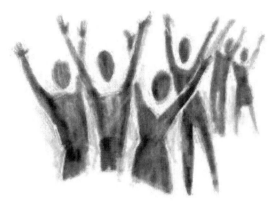

*I will therefore that men pray every where, lifting up holy hands, without wrath and doubting (**I Timothy 2:8**). Neither give place to the devil (**Ephesians 4:27**).*

How you want people to know you, is by your first show. A second time, you may not get to shine.

*Let your light so shine before men, that they may see your good works, and glorify your Father which is in heaven (**Matthew 5:16**). Remember therefore from whence thou art fallen, and repent, and do the first works; or else I will come unto thee quickly, and will remove thy candlestick out of his place, except thou repent (**Revelation 2:5**).*

Leave your worries at the cross, and present them to the Boss.

*Lord, how are they increased that trouble me! many are they that rise up against me. Many there be which say of my soul, There is no help for him in God. Selah. But thou, O LORD, art a shield for me; my glory, and the lifter up of mine head. I cried unto the LORD with my voice, and he heard me out of his holy hill. Selah. I laid me down and slept; I awaked; for the LORD sustained me. I will not be afraid of ten thousands of people, that have set themselves against me round about. Arise, O LORD; save me, O my God: for thou hast smitten all mine enemies upon the cheek bone; thou hast broken the teeth of the ungodly. Salvation belongeth unto the LORD: thy blessing is upon thy people. Selah **(Psalms 3:1-8)**. For in the time of trouble he shall hide me in his pavilion: in the secret of his tabernacle shall he hide me; he shall set me up upon a rock **(Psalm 27:5)**. The LORD will perfect that which concerneth me: thy mercy, O LORD, endureth for ever: forsake not the works of thine own hands **(Psalm 138:8)**.*

You will have what you say, especially when you pray.

Jesus answered and said unto them, Verily I say unto you, If ye have faith, and doubt not, ye shall not only do this which is done to the fig tree, but also if ye shall say unto this mountain, Be thou removed, and be thou cast into the sea; it shall be done. And all things, whatsoever ye shall ask in prayer, believing, ye shall receive **(Matthew 21:21-22)**.

You have to have the faith to get through it for God to do it.

*Now faith is the substance of things hoped for, the evidence of things not seen **(Hebrews 11:1)**. But without faith it is impossible to please him: for he that cometh to God must believe that he is, and that he is a rewarder of them that diligently seek him **(Hebrews 11:6)**.*

Negative feedback can result in a negative deed back.

> *Either make the tree good, and his fruit good; or else make the tree corrupt, and his fruit corrupt: for the tree is known by his fruit. O generation of vipers, how can ye, being evil, speak good things? for out of the abundance of the heart the mouth speaketh. A good man out of the good treasure of the heart bringeth forth good things: and an evil man out of the evil treasure bringeth forth evil things. But I say unto you, That every idle word that men shall speak, they shall give account thereof in the day of judgment. For by thy words thou shalt be justified, and by thy words thou shalt be condemned* **(Matthew 12:33-37)**.

The Lord said that He'll be with you from the beginning to the end, and if you'll be on His team, He'll give you a different spin, and you'll always win.

> *And he said unto me, It is done. I am Alpha and Omega, the beginning and the end. I will give unto him that is athirst of the fountain of the water of life freely* **(Revelation 21:6)**. *What shall we then say to these things? If God be for us, who can be against us* **(Romans 8:31)**. *I am Alpha and Omega, the beginning and the ending, saith the Lord, which is, and which was, and which is to come, the Almighty* **(Revelation 1:8)**.

The devil can try to block me, but he can't stop me.

*And that they may recover themselves out of the snare of the devil, who are taken captive by him at his will **(II Timothy 2:26)**. Nay, in all these things we are more than conquerors through him that loved us **(Romans 8:37)**.*

A yoke beater is a yoke defeater.

*And it shall come to pass in that day, that his burden shall be taken away from off thy shoulder, and his yoke from off thy neck, and the yoke shall be destroyed because of the anointing **(Isaiah 10:27)**. Stand fast therefore in the liberty wherewith Christ hath made us free, and be not entangled again with the yoke of bondage **(Galatians 5:1)**.*

Good things come to those who wait, and nothing comes to those who hate.

> *Whoso loveth instruction loveth knowledge: but he that hateth reproof is brutish. A good man obtaineth favour of the LORD: but a man of wicked devices will he condemn. A man shall not be established by wickedness: but the root of the righteous shall not be moved* **(Proverbs 12:1-3)**. *Our soul waiteth for the LORD: he is our help and our shield. For our heart shall rejoice in him, because we have trusted in his holy name. Let thy mercy, O LORD, be upon us, according as we hope in thee* **(Psalms 33:20-22)**. *Wait on the LORD: be of good courage, and he shall strengthen thine heart: wait, I say, on the LORD* **(Psalm 27:14)**.

Do what the Lord tells you to do. You will need Him to get you through.

> *Blessed are they that do his commandments, that they may have right to the tree of life, and may enter in through the gates into the city* **(Revelation 22:14)**. *I will instruct thee and teach thee in the way which thou shalt go: I will guide thee with mine eye* **(Psalm 32:8)**. *In all thy ways acknowledge him, and he shall direct thy paths* **(Proverbs 3:6)**.

When you give God the glory, He will change your whole life story.

*And he said, I beseech thee, shew me thy glory. And he said, I will make all my goodness pass before thee, and I will proclaim the name of the LORD before thee; and will be gracious to whom I will be gracious, and will shew mercy on whom I will shew mercy (**Exodus 33:18-19**).*

In our Heavenly Father we say "Yes!", and not to man of flesh.

*It is better to trust in the LORD than to put confidence in man (**Psalm 118:8**). For we are the circumcision, which worship God in the spirit, and rejoice in Christ Jesus, and have no confidence in the flesh (**Philippians 3:3**).*

The good Lord's shine in me will overtake Satan blinding me.

*And they that be wise shall shine as the brightness of the firmament; and they that turn many to righteousness as the stars for ever and ever **(Daniel 12:3)**. But he that hateth his brother is in darkness, and walketh in darkness, and knoweth not whither he goeth, because that darkness hath blinded his eyes **(I John 2:11)**.*

All things can be a "Yes I Can" with an "Amen!"

*But Jesus beheld them, and said unto them, With men this is impossible; but with God all things are possible **(Matthew 19:26)**. Jesus said unto him, If thou canst believe, all things are possible to him that believeth **(Mark 9:23)**. And he said, The things which are impossible with men are possible with God **(Luke 18:27)**.*

Wisdom is the key and the Lord gives it to us free.

*Happy is the man that findeth wisdom, and the man that getteth understanding **(Proverbs 3:13)**. Wisdom is the principal thing; therefore get wisdom: and with all thy getting get understanding **(Proverbs 4:7)**. If any of you lack wisdom, let him ask of God, that giveth to all men liberally, and upbraideth not; and it shall be given him **(James 1:5)**.*

When you pray in the spirit, always do it in the name of Jesus, but by no means, don't give blame to Jesus.

*But ye, beloved, building up yourselves on your most holy faith, praying in the Holy Ghost **(Jude 1:20)**. Praying always with all prayer and supplication in the Spirit, and watching thereunto with all perseverance and supplication for all saints **(Ephesians 6:18)**.*

The Lord gives us freedom for the key to His kingdom.

*For so an entrance shall be ministered unto you abundantly into the everlasting kingdom of our Lord and Saviour Jesus Christ **(II Peter 1:11)**. Wherefore we receiving a kingdom which cannot be moved, let us have grace, whereby we may serve God acceptably with reverence and godly fear: For our God is a consuming fire **(Hebrews 12:28-29)**. Thine, O LORD is the greatness, and the power, and the glory, and the victory, and the majesty: for all that is in the heaven and in the earth is thine; thine is the kingdom, OLORD, and thou art exalted as head above all **(I Chronicles 29:11)**.*

Use your talents as a Christian base, and don't let it go to waste.

*A man's gift maketh room for him, and bringeth him before great men **(Proverbs 18:16)**. And whatsoever ye do, do it heartily, as to the Lord, and not unto men; Knowing that of the Lord ye shall receive the reward of the inheritance: for ye serve the Lord Christ **(Colossians 3:23-24)**.*

When you thirst for the word, you can't just drink of one verse.

In the last day, that great day of the feast, Jesus stood and cried, saying, If any man thirst, let him come unto me, and drink. He that believeth on me, as the scripture hath said, out of his belly shall flow rivers of living water **(John 7:37-38)**.

If you don't practice what you preach, you need to change your speech!

No man can serve two masters: for either he will hate the one, and love the other; or else he will hold to the one, and despise the other. Ye cannot serve God and mammon **(Matthew 6:24)**.

The word is more precious than silver and gold, and we should love it with all our hearts and souls.

*How much better is it to get wisdom than gold! and to get understanding rather to be chosen than silver (**Proverbs 16:16**)! The law of the LORD is perfect, converting the soul: the testimony of the LORD is sure, making wise the simple. The statutes of the LORD are right, rejoicing the heart: the commandment of the LORD is pure, enlightening the eyes. The fear of the LORD is clean, enduring for ever: the judgments of the LORD are true and righteous altogether. More to be desired are they than gold, yea, than much fine gold: sweeter also than honey and the honeycomb (**Psalms 19:7-10**).*

Satan will show up in your spirit, only if you will allow him in it.

*Be not hasty in thy spirit to be angry: for anger resteth in the bosom of fools (**Ecclesiastes 7:9**).*

Come rooted and suited or get booted. Here are a few ways to get booted:

A

B

A. *By getting kicked out.*

B. *By getting your car booted.*

In picture "A", he is Kicked out of the premises.

In picture "B", a boot is on the car with no where to go.

That Christ may dwell in your hearts by faith; that ye, being rooted and grounded in love **(Ephesians 3:17)**. *Rooted and built up in him, and stablished in the faith, as ye have been taught, abounding therein with thanksgiving* **(Colossians 2:7)**.

If you speak negative from your mouth, you will dig yourself devil south. But, if you let the Lord control what you say, everything will be okay.

Death and life are in the power of the tongue: and they that love it shall eat the fruit thereof **(Proverbs 18:21)**.

By your faith, God takes away all of the guess work, and turns it into your blessed works.

*And Isaac intreated the LORD for his wife, because she was barren: and the LORD was intreated of him, and Rebekah his wife conceived. And the children struggled together within her; and she said, If it be so, why am I thus? And she went to enquire of the LORD. And the LORD said unto her, Two nations are in thy womb, and two manner of people shall be separated from thy bowels; and the one people shall be stronger than the other people; and the elder shall serve the younger. And when her days to be delivered were fulfilled, behold, there were twins in her womb. And the first came out red, all over like an hairy garment; and they called his name Esau. And after that came his brother out, and his hand took hold on Esau's heel; and his name was called Jacob: and Isaac was threescore years old when she bare them **(Genesis 25:21-26)**.*

If God lives within you, He can make things through you.

*For every house is builded by some man; but he that built all things is God **(Hebrews 3:4)**.*

To keep worry off your life story, The Lord will give you a mission for His glory.

Therefore I say unto you, Take no thought for your life, what ye shall eat, or what ye shall drink; nor yet for your body, what ye shall put on. Is not the life more than meat, and the body than raiment? Behold the fowls of the air: for they sow not, neither do they reap, nor gather into barns; yet your heavenly Father feedeth them. Are ye not much better than they? Which of you by taking thought can add one cubit unto his stature? And why take ye thought for raiment? Consider the lilies of the field, how they grow; they toil not, neither do they spin: And yet I say unto you, That even Solomon in all his glory was not arrayed like one of these. Wherefore, if God so clothe the grass of the field, which to day is, and to morrow is cast into the oven, shall he not much more clothe you, O ye of little faith? Therefore take no thought, saying, What shall we eat? or, What shall we drink? or, Wherewithal shall we be clothed
(Matthew 6:25-31)?

In His word I will abide, because there is no better place to reside.

Lord, thou hast been our dwelling place in all generations **(Psalm 90:1)**. *He that dwelleth in the secret place of the most High shall abide under the shadow of the Almighty* **(Psalm 91:1)**. *Then said Jesus to those Jews which believed on him, If ye continue in my word, then are ye my disciples indeed; And ye shall know the truth, and the truth shall make you free* **(John 8:31-32)**.

When you have faith in Jesus, the Son, through His power, the victory is already won.

For whatsoever is born of God overcometh the world: and this is the victory that overcometh the world, even our faith **(I John 5:4)**. *But thanks be to God, which giveth us the victory through our Lord Jesus Christ* **(I Corinthians 15:57)**.

If you stay strong in the Lord, you will overcome your denials, when you have grace from God, you will go beyond your trials.

By faith, you will overcome.
Moreover, with God, you can overcome
any hurdle in life.

*For whatsoever is born of God overcometh the world: and this is the victory that overcometh the world, even our faith **(I John 5:4)**. He that hath an ear, let him hear what the Spirit saith unto the churches; To him that overcometh will I give to eat of the tree of life, which is in the midst of the paradise of God **(Revelation 2:7)**.*

Whatever a man sows through, he also goes through.

*Be not deceived; God is not mocked: for whatsoever a man soweth, that shall he also reap. For he that soweth to his flesh shall of the flesh reap corruption; but he that soweth to the Spirit shall of the Spirit reap life everlasting **(Galatians 6:7-8)**.*

If you love it, make sure that God's above it.

*And God spake all these words, saying, I am the L*ORD *thy God, which have brought thee out of the land of Egypt, out of the house of bondage. Thou shalt have no other gods before me. Thou shalt not make unto thee any graven image, or any likeness of any thing that is in heaven above, or that is in the earth beneath, or that is in the water under the earth. Thou shalt not bow down thyself to them, nor serve them: for I the L*ORD *thy God am a jealous God, visiting the iniquity of the fathers upon the children unto the third and fourth generation of them that hate me; And shewing mercy unto thousands of them that love me, and keep my commandments (Exodus 20:1-6).*

We have to stand strong through our faith and our praise, to escort a way out of this tormented maze.

*Whereby are given unto us exceeding great and precious promises: that by these ye might be partakers of the divine nature, having escaped the corruption that is in the world through lust (II Peter 1:4). Therefore, my beloved brethren, be ye stedfast, unmoveable, always abounding in the work of the Lord, forasmuch as ye know that your labour is not in vain in the Lord (I Corinthians 15:58). Great is the L*ORD*, and greatly to be praised; and his greatness is unsearchable (Psalm 145:3).*

There's no crime in the design of spiritual new wine.

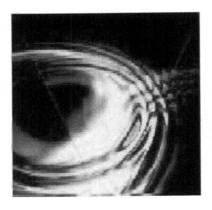

And it shall come to pass in that day, that the mountains shall drop down new wine, and the hills shall flow with milk, and all the rivers of Judah shall flow with waters, and a fountain shall come forth out of the house of the LORD, and shall water the valley of Shittim **(Joel 3:18)**. *For how great is his goodness, and how great is his beauty! corn shall make the young men cheerful, and new wine the maids* **(Zechariah 9:17)**. *Neither do men put new wine into old bottles: else the bottles break, and the wine runneth out, and the bottles perish: but they put new wine into new bottles, and both are preserved* **(Matthew 9:17)**.

Knowledge is power for this Holy Ghost hour.

A wise man is strong; yea, a man of knowledge increaseth strength **(Proverbs 24:5)**.

God can turnaround what's pathetic in your life to make it perfected in your life.

> But as for you, ye thought evil against me; but God meant it unto good, to bring to pass, as it is this day, to save much people alive **(Genesis 50:20)**. And we know that all things work together for good to them that love God, to them who are the called according to his purpose **(Romans 8:28)**.

To God be the glory when you hear the revelation of His story that is working through your mind as His glory will make you shine.

> Delight thyself also in the LORD: and he shall give thee the desires of thine heart **(Psalm 37:4)**. Arise, shine; for thy light is come, and the glory of the LORD is risen upon thee **(Isaiah 60:1)**. Let your light so shine before men, that they may see your good works, and glorify your Father which is in heaven **(Matthew 5:16)**.

To have a good relationship, you must have patientship.

*With all lowliness and meekness, with longsuffering, forbearing one another in love **(Ephesians 4:2)**. Wives, submit yourselves unto your own husbands, as unto the Lord. For the husband is the head of the wife, even as Christ is the head of the church: and he is the saviour of the body. Therefore as the church is subject unto Christ, so let the wives be to their own husbands in every thing. Husbands, love your wives, even as Christ also loved the church, and gave himself for it; That he might sanctify and cleanse it with the washing of water by the word, That he might present it to himself a glorious church, not having spot, or wrinkle, or any such thing; but that it should be holy and without blemish. So ought men to love their wives as their own bodies. He that loveth his wife loveth himself. For no man ever yet hated his own flesh; but nourisheth and cherisheth it, even as the Lord the church: For we are members of his body, of his flesh, and of his bones. For this cause shall a man leave his father and mother, and shall be joined unto his wife, and they two shall be one flesh. This is a great mystery: but I speak concerning Christ and the church. Nevertheless let every one of you in particular so love his wife even as himself; and the wife see that she reverence her husband **(Ephesians 5:22-33)**.*

When you're unplugged you can't be bugged. There are times that you have to pause for the cause, because you don't know the alls.

And I will give peace in the land, and ye shall lie down, and none shall make you afraid: and I will rid evil beasts out of the land, neither shall the sword go through your land. And ye shall chase your enemies, and they shall fall before you by the sword **(Leviticus 26:6-7)**. *For this cause we also, since the day we heard it, do not cease to pray for you, and to desire that ye might be filled with the knowledge of his will in all wisdom and spiritual understanding; That ye might walk worthy of the Lord unto all pleasing, being fruitful in every good work, and increasing in the knowledge of God; Strengthened with all might, according to his glorious power, unto all patience and longsuffering with joyfulness* **(Colossians 1:9-11)**.

When you rest in the Lord, in Heaven awaits your greatest reward.

For the hope which is laid up for you in heaven, whereof ye heard before in the word of the truth of the gospel; Which is come unto you, as it is in all the world; and bringeth forth fruit, as it doth also in you, since the day ye heard of it, and knew the grace of God in truth **(Colossians 1:5-6)**. *Rejoice, and be exceeding glad: for great is your reward in heaven: for so persecuted they the prophets which were before you* **(Matthew 5:12)**.

Every chain that the devil makes, the Lord gives us the power to break.

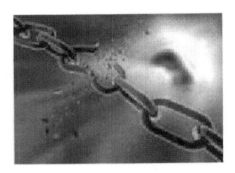

*For the weapons of our warfare are not carnal, but mighty through God to the pulling down of strong holds **(II Corinthians 10:4)**. No weapon that is formed against thee shall prosper; and every tongue that shall rise against thee in judgment thou shalt condemn. This is the heritage of the servants of the LORD, and their righteousness is of me, saith the LORD **(Isaiah 54:17)**.*

Temptation is strong when you know it's wrong.

*There hath no temptation taken you but such as is common to man: but God is faithful, who will not suffer you to be tempted above that ye are able; but will with the temptation also make a way to escape, that ye may be able to bear it **(I Corinthians 10:13)**.*

Have belief and patience in God, and don't put on a facade.

> *Knowing this, that the trying of your faith worketh patience. But let patience have her perfect work, that ye may be perfect and entire, wanting nothing. If any of you lack wisdom, let him ask of God, that giveth to all men liberally, and upbraideth not; and it shall be given him. But let him ask in faith, nothing wavering. For he that wavereth is like a wave of the sea driven with the wind and tossed. For let not that man think that he shall receive any thing of the Lord. A double minded man is unstable in all his ways* **(James 1:3-8)**.

When you submit yourself, and you speak boldly God's word, the devil will flee like a bird.

> *Submit yourselves therefore to God. Resist the devil, and he will flee from you* **(James 4:7)**.

If you let the devil shake you, he'll bake you. You should be stirred in God's word and not by what Satan serves.

Then was Jesus led up of the Spirit into the wilderness to be tempted of the devil. And when he had fasted forty days and forty nights, he was afterward an hungred. And when the tempter came to him, he said, If thou be the Son of God, command that these stones be made bread. But he answered and said, It is written, Man shall not live by bread alone, but by every word that proceedeth out of the mouth of God. Then the devil taketh him up into the holy city, and setteth him on a pinnacle of the temple, And saith unto him, If thou be the Son of God, cast thyself down: for it is written, He shall give his angels charge concerning thee: and in their hands they shall bear thee up, lest at any time thou dash thy foot against a stone. Jesus said unto him, It is written again, Thou shalt not tempt the Lord thy God. Again, the devil taketh him up into an exceeding

high mountain, and sheweth him all the kingdoms of the world, and the glory of them; And saith unto him, All these things will I give thee, if thou wilt fall down and worship me. Then saith Jesus unto him, Get thee hence, Satan: for it is written, Thou shalt worship the Lord thy God, and him only shalt thou serve **(Matthew 4:1-10)**.

Don't let sin be your friend, because you won't win.

Ye adulterers and adulteresses, know ye not that the friendship of the world is enmity with God? whosoever therefore will be a friend of the world is the enemy of God **(James 4:4)**. *For the wages of sin is death; but the gift of God is eternal life through Jesus Christ our Lord* **(Romans 6:23)**.

Don't let the devil win, because he's not here to be your friend. He will try to make you sin, so don't let him have you pinned.

Pull me out of the net that they have laid privily for me: for thou art my strength **(Psalm 31:4)**. *Whosoever committeth sin transgresseth also the law: for sin is the transgression of the law. And ye know that he was manifested to take away our sins; and in him is no sin. Whosoever abideth in him sinneth not: whosoever sinneth hath not seen him, neither known him. Little children, let no man deceive you: he that doeth righteousness is righteous, even as he is righteous. He that committeth sin is of the devil; for the devil sinneth from the beginning. For this purpose the Son of God was manifested, that he might destroy the works of the devil. Whosoever is born of God doth not commit sin; for his seed remaineth in him: and he cannot sin, because he is born of God* **(I John 3:4-9)**. *Submit yourselves therefore to God. Resist the devil, and he will flee from you* **(James 4:7)**.

Knock on the Lord's door and He will open up His shore. Knock on His door through prayer, and He will show you His care.

When you put your trust in God, He will
Give you an overflow of blessings.

Ask, and it shall be given you; seek, and ye shall find; knock, and it shall be opened unto you: For every one that asketh receiveth; and he that seeketh findeth; and to him that knocketh it shall be opened **(Matthew 7:7-8)***. He that believeth on me, as the scripture hath said, out of his belly shall flow rivers of living water* **(John 7:38)***.*

The more you share, the more you prove your care.

Give, and it shall be given unto you; good measure, pressed down, and shaken together, and running over, shall men give into your bosom. For with the same measure that ye mete withal it shall be measured to you again **(Luke 6:38)***. But to do good and to communicate forget not: for with such sacrifices God is well pleased* **(Hebrews 13:16)***.*

The devil is so cursiful, but our Lord is so merciful.

For as many as are of the works of the law are under the curse: for it is written, Cursed is every one that continueth not in all things which are written in the book of the law to do them. But that no man is justified by the law in the sight of God, it is evident: for, The just shall live by faith. And the law is not of faith: but, The man that doeth them shall live in them. Christ hath redeemed us from the curse of the law, being made a curse for us: for it is written, Cursed is every one that hangeth on a tree: That the blessing of Abraham might come on the Gentiles through Jesus Christ; that we might receive the promise of the Spirit through faith (Galatians 3:10-14). Behold, we count them happy which endure. Ye have heard of the patience of Job, and have seen the end of the Lord; that the Lord is very pitiful, and of tender mercy (James 5:11).

Don't have the spirit of fear, have the spirit of cheer.

Yea, though I walk through the valley of the shadow of death, I will fear no evil: for thou art with me; thy rod and thy staff they comfort me. Thou preparest a table before me in the presence of mine enemies: thou anointest my head with oil; my cup runneth over. Surely goodness and mercy shall follow me all the days of my life: and I will dwell in the house of the LORD for ever (Psalms 23:4-6).

The Lord said to give Him a Hallelujah, and He will open doors that will out do yah.

> *I know thy works: behold, I have set before thee an open door, and no man can shut it: for thou hast a little strength, and hast kept my word, and hast not denied my name **(Revelation 3:8)**. And after these things I heard a great voice of much people in heaven, saying, Alleluia; Salvation, and glory, and honour, and power, unto the Lord our God: For true and righteous are his judgments: for he hath judged the great whore, which did corrupt the earth with her fornication, and hath avenged the blood of his servants at her hand. And again they said, Alleluia And her smoke rose up for ever and ever. And the four and twenty elders and the four beasts fell down and worshipped God that sat on the throne, saying, Amen; Alleluia. And a voice came out of the throne, saying, Praise our God, all ye his servants, and ye that fear him, both small and great. And I heard as it were the voice of a great multitude, and as the voice of many waters, and as the voice of mighty thunderings, saying, Alleluia: for the Lord God omnipotent reigneth **(Revelations 19:1-6)**.*

Use your tongue to work against the devil, in going to the next level.

> *Keep thy tongue from evil, and thy lips from speaking guile **(Psalm 34:13)**. Let him eschew evil, and do good; let him seek peace, and ensue it **(I Peter 3:11)**.*

Do a Holy Ghost dance, and don't give the devil a chance. Do it in the spirit, so your Heavenly Father can hear it.

*Praise him with the timbrel and dance: praise him with stringed instruments and organs **(Psalm 150:4)**. Make a joyful noise unto the* LORD, *all the earth: make a loud noise, and rejoice, and sing praise. Sing unto the* LORD *with the harp; with the harp, and the voice of a psalm. With trumpets and sound of cornet make a joyful noise before the* LORD, *the King **(Psalms 98:4-6)**. Put on the whole armour of God, that ye may be able to stand against the wiles of the devil. For we wrestle not against flesh and blood, but against principalities, against powers, against the rulers of the darkness of this world, against spiritual wickedness in high places **(Ephesians 6:11-12)**.*

It's better to hear good news over bad blues.

He that hath an ear, let him hear what the Spirit saith unto the churches; To him that overcometh will I give to eat of the tree of life, which is in the midst of the paradise of God **(Revelation 2:7)**. *Redeeming the time, because the days are evil* **(Ephesians 5:16)**. *Let no man deceive you with vain words: for because of these things cometh the wrath of God upon the children of disobedience* **(Ephesians 5:6)**. *Then shall the righteous shine forth as the sun in the kingdom of their Father. Who hath ears to hear, let him hear* **(Matthew 13:43)**. *The Lord gives us access to His kingdom. All we have to do is lean to Him. The* LORD *hath prepared his throne in the heavens; and his kingdom ruleth over all* **(Psalm 103:19)**. *Trust in the* LORD *with all thine heart; and lean not unto thine own understanding. In all thy ways acknowledge him, and he shall direct thy paths* **(Proverbs 3:5-6)**. *By whom also we have access by faith into this grace wherein we stand, and rejoice in hope of the glory of God* **(Romans 5:2)**.

When I have a testimony (through God's grace), none are phony.

Thy testimonies are very sure: holiness becometh thine house, O LORD, *for ever* **(Psalm 93:5)**.

When you're out in the sun, the day is still young. When the moon is whole, the day is old.

 VS

The sun shall not smite thee by day, nor the moon by night **(Psalm 121:6)**.

Don't be confused, it's all divine news. If we abide by the Lord's grace, there's no way to lose.

For God is not the author of confusion, but of peace, as in all churches of the saints **(I Corinthians 14:33)**. *According as his divine power hath given unto us all things that pertain unto life and godliness, through the knowledge of him that hath called us to glory and virtue:* **(II Peter 1:3)**. *He that dwelleth in the secret place of the most High shall abide under the shadow of the Almighty. I will say of the* LORD, *He is my refuge and my fortress: my God; in him will I trust* **(Psalms 91:1-2)**.

Do a Hallelujah praise for His glory, and tell your testimonial story. Sometimes, you can't get your story out, so you have to digest it with a shout.

> *And they overcame him by the blood of the Lamb, and by the word of their testimony; and they loved not their lives unto the death **(Revelation 12:11)**. Make a joyful noise unto the LORD, all the earth: make a loud noise, and rejoice, and sing praise **(Psalm 98:4)**.*

Let's do a dance and shout, and let the devil know what we're all about.

*Make a joyful noise unto the LORD, all ye lands **(Psalm 100:1)**. Let them praise his name in the dance: let them sing praises unto him with the timbrel and harp **(Psalm 149:3)**.*

I may go into an overflow,

because God's grace is an endless road.

Thou preparest a table before me in the presence of mine enemies: thou anointest my head with oil; my cup runneth over. Surely goodness and mercy shall follow me all the days of my life: and I will dwell in the house of the LORD for ever ***(Psalms 23:5-6)***.

You're nobody until somebody hates you, but know that it's God who awaits you.

Ye have heard that it hath been said, Thou shalt love thy neighbour, and hate thine enemy. But I say unto you, Love your enemies, bless them that curse you, do good to them that hate you, and pray for them which despitefully use you, and persecute you; That ye may be the children of your Father which is in heaven: for he maketh his sun to rise on the evil and on the good, and sendeth rain on the just and on the unjust **(Matthew 5:43-45)**. *And therefore will the* LORD *wait, that he may be gracious unto you, and therefore will he be exalted, that he may have mercy upon you: for the* LORD *is a God of judgment: blessed are all they that wait for him* **(Isaiah 30:18)**.

What everyone resents, to God you present your repents.

Then Peter said unto them, Repent, and be baptized every one of you in the name of Jesus Christ for the remission of sins, and ye shall receive the gift of the Holy Ghost **(Acts 2:38)**.

If you can succeed through your mind, you will never go spiritually blind.

*That the righteousness of the law might be fulfilled in us, who walk not after the flesh, but after the Spirit. For they that are after the flesh do mind the things of the flesh; but they that are after the Spirit the things of the Spirit. For to be carnally minded is death; but to be spiritually minded is life and peace. Because the carnal mind is enmity against God: for it is not subject to the law of God, neither indeed can be. So then they that are in the flesh cannot please God. But ye are not in the flesh, but in the Spirit, if so be that the Spirit of God dwell in you. Now if any man have not the Spirit of Christ, he is none of his **(Romans 8:4-9)**. In whom the god of this world hath blinded the minds of them which believe not, lest the light of the glorious gospel of Christ, who is the image of God, should shine unto them **(II Corinthians 4:4)**. And I will bring the blind by a way that they knew not; I will lead them in paths that they have not known: I will make darkness light before them, and crooked things straight. These things will I do unto them, and not forsake them **(Isaiah 42:16)**.*

You have to fix your dents in life where you need confidence in life.

*Cast not away therefore your confidence, which hath great recompence of reward. For ye have need of patience, that, after ye have done the will of God, ye might receive the promise **(Hebrews 10:35-36)**.*

Don't get delirious, because life is not that serious.

Come, ye children, hearken unto me: I will teach you the fear of the LORD. What man is he that desireth life, and loveth many days, that he may see good? Keep thy tongue from evil, and thy lips from speaking guile. Depart from evil, and do good; seek peace, and pursue it **(Psalms 34:11-14)**. *In my distress I cried unto the LORD, and he heard me. Deliver my soul, O LORD, from lying lips, and from a deceitful tongue. What shall be given unto thee? or what shall be done unto thee, thou false tongue? Sharp arrows of the mighty, with coals of juniper. Woe is me, that I sojourn in Mesech, that I dwell in the tents of Kedar! My soul hath long dwelt with him that hateth peace. I am for peace: but when I speak, they are for war* **(Psalms 120:1-7)**. *I will lift up mine eyes unto the hills, from whence cometh my help. My help cometh from the LORD, which made heaven and earth. He will not suffer thy foot to be moved: he that keepeth thee will not slumber. Behold, he that keepeth Israel shall neither slumber nor sleep. The LORD is thy keeper: the LORD is thy shade upon thy right hand. The sun shall not smite thee by day, nor the moon by night. The LORD shall preserve thee from all evil: he shall preserve thy soul. The LORD shall preserve thy going out and thy coming in from this time forth, and even for evermore* **(Psalms 121:1-8)**.

We are made in the image of God, and we have no limits from God.

So God created man in his own image, in the image of God created he him; male and female created he them **(Genesis 1:27)**. *Now unto him that is able to do exceeding abundantly above all that we ask or think, according to the power that worketh in us,* **(Ephesians 3:20)**. *For as the heavens are higher than the earth, so are my ways higher than your ways, and my thoughts than your thoughts* **(Isaiah 55:9)**.

When you embed your gift to God, He will not cease to increase.

I have planted, Apollos watered; but God gave the increase. So then neither is he that planteth any thing, neither he that watereth; but God that giveth the increase. Now he that planteth and he that watereth are one: and every man shall receive his own reward according to his own labour. For we are labourers together with God: ye are God's husbandry, ye are God's building. According to the grace of God which is given unto me, as a wise masterbuilder, I have laid the foundation, and another buildeth thereon. But let every man take heed how he buildeth thereupon. For other foundation can no man lay than that is laid, which is Jesus Christ. If any man's work abide which he hath built thereupon, he shall receive a reward **(I Corinthians 3:6-11, 14)**.

Satan operates with his imps that are assigned as his temps. Remember, troubles don't last always.

> ➢ Imp is defined as a little devil or demon; an evil spirit.

*For I reckon that the sufferings of this present time are not worthy to be compared with the glory which shall be revealed in us (**Romans 8:18**). I love the LORD, because he hath heard my voice and my supplications. Because he hath inclined his ear unto me, therefore will I call upon him as long as I live. The sorrows of death compassed me, and the pains of hell gat hold upon me: I found trouble and sorrow. Then called I upon the name of the LORD; O LORD, I beseech thee, deliver my soul. Gracious is the LORD, and righteous; yea, our God is merciful. The LORD preserveth the simple: I was brought low, and he helped me (**Psalms 116:1-6**).*

When it comes to God, you can't rush Him, you can't hush Him, you can't fuss at Him, all you can do is trust Him.

> *Trust in the L*ORD *with all thine heart; and lean not unto thine own understanding* **(Proverbs 3:5)**. *But if we hope for that we see not, then do we with patience wait for it* **(Romans 8:25)**. *Wait on the L*ORD*: be of good courage, and he shall strengthen thine heart: wait, I say, on the L*ORD **(Psalm 27:14)**.

Speak the word out loud, in a crowd, and be proud under the Lord's vows.

> *But when they deliver you up, take no thought how or what ye shall speak: for it shall be given you in that same hour what ye shall speak. For it is not ye that speak, but the Spirit of your Father which speaketh in you* **(Matthew 10:19-20)**. *Howbeit when he, the Spirit of truth, is come, he will guide you into all truth: for he shall not speak of himself; but whatsoever he shall hear, that shall he speak: and he will shew you things to come* **(John 16:13)**. *Vow, and pay unto the L*ORD *your God: let all that be round about him bring presents unto him that ought to be feared* **(Psalm 76:11)**. *In God we boast all the day long, and praise thy name for ever. Selah* **(Psalm 44:8)**.

A wave after wave of blessing in your life should be a wave after wave of praise.

Bless the LORD, O my soul: and all that is within me, bless his holy name. Bless the LORD, O my soul, and forget not all his benefits: Who forgiveth all thine iniquities; who healeth all thy diseases; Who redeemeth thy life from destruction; who crowneth thee with lovingkindness and tender mercies; Who satisfieth thy mouth with good things; so that thy youth is renewed like the eagle's **(Psalms 103:1-5)**. *By him therefore let us offer the sacrifice of praise to God continually, that is, the fruit of our lips giving thanks to his name* **(Hebrews 13:15)**.

Give yourself a break, and open God's word and meditate. Things will flow like rivers of water, and they will be less harder.

*But his delight is in the law of the LORD; and in his law doth he meditate day and night **(Psalm 1:2)**. And he shewed me a pure river of water of life, clear as crystal, proceeding out of the throne of God and of the Lamb. In the midst of the street of it, and on either side of the river, was there the tree of life, which bare twelve manner of fruits, and yielded her fruit every month: and the leaves of the tree were for the healing of the nations **(Revelations 22:1-2)**.*

When you have hope in the Lord, He will open all doors.

*I know thy works: behold, I have set before thee an open door, and no man can shut it: for thou hast a little strength, and hast kept my word, and hast not denied my name **(Revelation 3:8)**.*

When Jesus gives the blind eyes to see, the devil only have wings to flee.

> *Therefore seeing we have this ministry, as we have received mercy, we faint not; But have renounced the hidden things of dishonesty, not walking in craftiness, nor handling the word of God deceitfully; but by manifestation of the truth commending ourselves to every man's conscience in the sight of God. But if our gospel be hid, it is hid to them that are lost: In whom the god of this world hath blinded the minds of them which believe not, lest the light of the glorious gospel of Christ, who is the image of God, should shine unto them **(II Corinthians 4:1-4)**. Submit yourselves therefore to God. Resist the devil, and he will flee from you **(James 4:7)**.*

Looks can be deceiving, but blessing are receiving.

> *And he cometh to Bethsaida; and they bring a blind man unto him, and besought him to touch him. And he took the blind man by the hand, and led him out of the town; and when he had spit on his eyes, and put his hands upon him, he asked him if he saw ought. And he looked up, and said, I see men as trees, walking. After that he put his hands again upon his eyes, and made him look up: and he was restored, and saw every man clearly **(Mark 8:22-25)**.*

Give God the highest praise, and perform it day by day.

> *Because thy lovingkindness is better than life, my lips shall praise thee. Thus will I bless thee while I live: I will lift up my hands in thy name. My soul shall be satisfied as with marrow and fatness; and my mouth shall praise thee with joyful lips: When I remember thee upon my bed, and meditate on thee in the night watches. Because thou hast been my help, therefore in the shadow of thy wings will I rejoice **(Psalms 63:3-7)**. I will sing unto the LORD as long as I live: I will sing praise to my God while I have my being. My meditation of him shall be sweet: I will be glad in the LORD **(Psalms 104:33-34)**. By him therefore let us offer the sacrifice of praise to God continually, that is, the fruit of our lips giving thanks to his name. But to do good and to communicate forget not: for with such sacrifices God is well pleased **(Hebrews 13:15-16)**. I will be glad and rejoice in thee: I will sing praise to thy name, O thou most High **(Psalm 9:2)**.*

Good things come to those who wait, and God's blessings are none for those who hate.

> *For evildoers shall be cut off: but those that wait upon the LORD, they shall inherit the earth **(Psalm 37:9)**. And I will bless them that bless thee, and curse him that curseth thee: and in thee shall all families of the earth be blessed **(Genesis 12:3)**.*

When people say bad things about you that are wrong, by God's will, you have to stay strong.

*Mine enemies speak evil of me, When shall he die, and his name perish (**Psalm 41:5**)? Deliver me from mine enemies, O my God: defend me from them that rise up against me (**Psalm 59:1**). Have not I commanded thee? Be strong and of a good courage; be not afraid, neither be thou dismayed: for the LORD thy God is with thee whithersoever thou goest (**Joshua 1:9**). Wherefore take unto you the whole armour of God, that ye may be able to withstand in the evil day, and having done all, to stand. Stand therefore, having your loins girt about with truth, and having on the breastplate of righteousness; And your feet shod with the preparation of the gospel of peace; Above all, taking the shield of faith, wherewith ye shall be able to quench all the fiery darts of the wicked (**Ephesians 6:13-16**).*

God's word is to be heard and not ignored.

*For unto us was the gospel preached, as well as unto them: but the word preached did not profit them, not being mixed with faith in them that heard it **(Hebrews 4:2)**. But be ye doers of the word, and not hearers only, deceiving your own selves. For if any be a hearer of the word, and not a doer, he is like unto a man beholding his natural face in a glass: For he beholdeth himself, and goeth his way, and straightway forgetteth what manner of man he was. But whoso looketh into the perfect law of liberty, and continueth therein, he being not a forgetful hearer, but a doer of the work, this man shall be blessed in his deed **(James 1:22-25)**.*

It's by your fruit, whom you have chosen to salute.

*Beware of false prophets, which come to you in sheep's clothing, but inwardly they are ravening wolves. Ye shall know them by their fruits. Do men gather grapes of thorns, or figs of thistles? Even so every good tree bringeth forth good fruit; but a corrupt tree bringeth forth evil fruit. A good tree cannot bring forth evil fruit, neither can a corrupt tree bring forth good fruit. Every tree that bringeth not forth good fruit is hewn down, and cast into the fire. Wherefore by their fruits ye shall know them **(Matthew 7:15-20)**.*

Have faith and believe in your Father, because He will take you farther.

> *And Jesus answering saith unto them,* Have faith in God. *For verily I say unto you, That whosoever shall say unto this mountain, Be thou removed, and be thou cast into the sea; and shall not doubt in his heart, but shall believe that those things which he saith shall come to pass; he shall have whatsoever he saith. Therefore I say unto you, What things soever ye desire, when ye pray, believe that ye receive them, and ye shall have them* **(Mark 11:22-24)**. *Therefore being justified by faith, we have peace with God through our Lord Jesus Christ: By whom also we have access by faith into this grace wherein we stand, and rejoice in hope of the glory of God* **(Romans 5:1-2)**.

Let no one take your joy, because Satan comes to kill, steal, and destroy.

> *Beloved, think it not strange concerning the fiery trial which is to try you, as though some strange thing happened unto you: But rejoice, inasmuch as ye are partakers of Christ's sufferings; that, when his glory shall be revealed, ye may be glad also with exceeding joy* **(I Peter 4:12-13)**. *The thief cometh not, but for to steal, and to kill, and to destroy: I am come that they might have life, and that they might have it more abundantly* **(John 10:10)**.

It's not what you try to produce in life, but it's about God's fruit in your life.

Ye shall know them by their fruits. Do men gather grapes of thorns, or figs of thistles? Even so every good tree bringeth forth good fruit; but a corrupt tree bringeth forth evil fruit **(Matthew 7:16-17)**. *I am the true vine, and my Father is the husbandman. Every branch in me that beareth not fruit he taketh away: and every branch that beareth fruit, he purgeth it, that it may bring forth more fruit. Now ye are clean through the word which I have spoken unto you. Abide in me, and I in you. As the branch cannot bear fruit of itself, except it abide in the vine; no more can ye, except ye abide in me. I am the vine, ye are the branches: He that abideth in me, and I in him, the same bringeth forth much fruit: for without me ye can do nothing. If a man abide not in me, he is cast forth as a branch, and is withered; and men gather them, and cast them into the fire, and they are burned. If ye abide in me, and my words abide in you, ye shall ask what ye will, and it shall be done unto you. Herein is my Father glorified, that ye bear much fruit; so shall ye be my disciples* **(John 15:1-8)**.

Give me the strength so that I can run that extra length.

He giveth power to the faint; and to them that have no might he increaseth strength ***(Isaiah 40:29)***. *God is my strength and power: and he maketh my way perfect. He maketh my feet like hinds' feet: and setteth me upon my high places. He teacheth my hands to war; so that a bow of steel is broken by mine arms. Thou hast also given me the shield of thy salvation: and thy gentleness hath made me great. Thou hast enlarged my steps under me; so that my feet did not slip* ***(II Samuel 22:33-37)***.

The Lord comes to your rescue, when Satan tries to get the best of you.

Because he hath set his love upon me, therefore will I deliver him: I will set him on high, because he hath known my name. He shall call upon me, and I will answer him: I will be with him in trouble; I will deliver him, and honour him ***(Psalms 91:14-15)***.

In the Lord, we come together in all decisions, so as brothers and sisters in Christ, let there be no divisions.

God is faithful, by whom ye were called unto the fellowship of his Son Jesus Christ our Lord. Now I beseech you, brethren, by the name of our Lord Jesus Christ, that ye all speak the same thing, and that there be no divisions among you; but that ye be perfectly joined together in the same mind and in the same judgment **(I Corinthians 1:9-10)**.

When God put your blessings on layaway, trust in Him by continuing to pray away / a way.

Pray without ceasing. In every thing give thanks: for this is the will of God in Christ Jesus concerning you **(I Thessalonians 5:17-18)**. *Trust in the LORD with all thine heart; and lean not unto thine own understanding. In all thy ways acknowledge him, and he shall direct thy paths* **(Proverbs 3:5-6)**.

238

Satan is not omnipresent, but the Lord wants His saints army present.

Thou therefore endure hardness, as a good soldier of Jesus Christ. No man that warreth entangleth himself with the affairs of this life; that he may please him who hath chosen him to be a soldier **(II Timothy 2:3-4)**. *Put on the whole armour of God, that ye may be able to stand against the wiles of the devil* **(Ephesians 6:11)**.

Give me a Hallelujah, and I'll throw it right back to ya.

Praise ye the LORD. Praise the LORD, O my soul. While I live will I praise the LORD: I will sing praises unto my God while I have any being **(Psalms 146:1-2)**. *Let the people praise thee, O God; let all the people praise thee. Then shall the earth yield her increase; and God, even our own God, shall bless us* **(Psalms 67:5-6)**.

When I have promises through God's grace, none can be erased.

> *Ye are the children of the prophets, and of the covenant which God made with our fathers, saying unto Abraham, And in thy seed shall all the kindreds of the earth be blessed* **(Acts 3:25)***. For all the promises of God in him are yea, and in him Amen, unto the glory of God by us* **(II Corinthians 1:20)***. Even as it is meet for me to think this of you all, because I have you in my heart; inasmuch as both in my bonds, and in the defence and confirmation of the gospel, ye all are partakers of my grace* **(Philippians 1:7)***. By whom also we have access by faith into this grace wherein we stand, and rejoice in hope of the glory of God* **(Romans 5:2)***.*

When you're in that flow, it's hard for that heavenly spirit to go.

> *I will bless the LORD at all times: his praise shall continually be in my mouth* **(Psalm 34:1)***. For it is impossible for those who were once enlightened, and have tasted of the heavenly gift, and were made partakers of the Holy Ghost, And have tasted the good word of God, and the powers of the world to come, If they shall fall away, to renew them again unto repentance; seeing they crucify to themselves the Son of God afresh, and put him to an open shame* **(Hebrews 6:4-6)***.*

God's thoughts are clean, and Satan's thoughts are mean. Therefore, to our Lord we pray, and give the devil no play.

*For my thoughts are not your thoughts, neither are your ways my ways, saith the LORD. For as the heavens are higher than the earth, so are my ways higher than your ways, and my thoughts than your thoughts **(Isaiah 55:8-9)**. For I know the thoughts that I think toward you, saith the LORD, thoughts of peace, and not of evil, to give you an expected end **(Jeremiah 29:11)**. Be sober, be vigilant; because your adversary the devil, as a roaring lion, walketh about, seeking whom he may devour **(I Peter 5:8)**: Lest Satan should get an advantage of us: for we are not ignorant of his devices **(II Corinthians 2:11)**. Hearken unto the voice of my cry, my King, and my God: for unto thee will I pray **(Psalm 5:2)**. Likewise the Spirit also helpeth our infirmities: for we know not what we should pray for as we ought: but the Spirit itself maketh intercession for us with groanings which cannot be uttered **(Romans 8:26)**. If my people, which are called by my name, shall humble themselves, and pray, and seek my face, and turn from their wicked ways; then will I hear from heaven, and will forgive their sin, and will heal their land **(II Chronicles 7:14)**. Neither give place to the devil **(Ephesians 4:27)**.*

Let your light shine day by day, by giving the Lord your best praise.

*Let your light so shine before men, that they may see your good works, and glorify your Father which is in heaven **(Matthew 5:16)**.*

God wants us to do more than adore Him to assure Him.

The words of the wise are as goads, and as nails fastened by the masters of assemblies, which are given from one shepherd. And further, by these, my son, be admonished: of making many books there is no end; and much study is a weariness of the flesh. Let us hear the conclusion of the whole matter: Fear God, and keep his commandments: for this is the whole duty of man. For God shall bring every work into judgment, with every secret thing, whether it be good, or whether it be evil **(Ecclesiastes 12:11-14)**.

In God's making, there's no faking.

Therefore if any man be in Christ, he is a new creature: old things are passed away; behold, all things are become new **(II Corinthians 5:17)**. *For the invisible things of him from the creation of the world are clearly seen, being understood by the things that are made, even his eternal power and Godhead; so that they are without excuse* **(Romans 1:20)**.

When your soul says yes (to God), you confess to be blessed.

And it shall come to pass, if thou shalt hearken diligently unto the voice of the LORD *thy God, to observe and to do all his commandments which I command thee this day, that the* LORD *thy God will set thee on high above all nations of the earth: And all these blessings shall come on thee, and overtake thee, if thou shalt hearken unto the voice of the* LORD *thy God* **(Deuteronomy 28:1-2)**.

Stop trying to compete, and work on yourself, so that you can be complete.

And whatsoever ye do in word or deed, do all in the name of the Lord Jesus, giving thanks to God and the Father by him **(Colossians 3:17)**. *For in him dwelleth all the fulness of the Godhead bodily. And ye are complete in him, which is the head of all principality and power* **(Colossians 2:9-10)**.

Your home should be your castle, and not a place to wrestle.

> *And Jesus knew their thoughts, and said unto them, Every kingdom divided against itself is brought to desolation; and every city or house divided against itself shall not stand: And if Satan cast out Satan, he is divided against himself; how shall then his kingdom stand? And if I by Beelzebub cast out devils, by whom do your children cast them out? therefore they shall be your judges. But if I cast out devils by the Spirit of God, then the kingdom of God is come unto you. Or else how can one enter into a strong man's house, and spoil his goods, except he first bind the strong man? and then he will spoil his house. He that is not with me is against me; and he that gathereth not with me scattereth abroad **(Matthew 12:25-30)**. Through wisdom is an house builded; and by understanding it is established: And by knowledge shall the chambers be filled with all precious and pleasant riches. A wise man is strong; yea, a man of knowledge increaseth strength **(Proverbs 24:3-5)**.*

God gives you seed for your sentimental need.

> *And he said, Unto you it is given to know the mysteries of the kingdom of God: but to others in parables; that seeing they might not see, and hearing they might not understand. Now the parable is this: The seed is the word of God **(Luke 8:10-11)**.*

People can't stop you from being promoted. The words that come out of your mouth, actions are quoted.

*Whoso keepeth his mouth and his tongue keepeth his soul from troubles **(Proverbs 21:23)**. A wholesome tongue is a tree of life: but perverseness therein is a breach in the spirit. A fool despiseth his father's instruction: but he that regardeth reproof is prudent. In the house of the righteous is much treasure: but in the revenues of the wicked is trouble. The lips of the wise disperse knowledge: but the heart of the foolish doeth not so. The sacrifice of the wicked is an abomination to the LORD: but the prayer of the upright is his delight. The way of the wicked is an abomination unto the LORD: but he loveth him that followeth after righteousness **(Proverbs 15:4-9)**. If any man among you seem to be religious, and bridleth not his tongue, but deceiveth his own heart, this man's religion is vain **(James 1:26)**. Be careful for nothing; but in every thing by prayer and supplication with thanksgiving let your requests be made known unto God **(Philippians 4:6)**.*

You are blessed to have your transgressions forgiven, and you can go on living.

*Blessed is he whose transgression is forgiven, whose sin is covered **(Psalm 32:1)**.*

245

When you give your soul to Christ, the devil won't treat you nice.

> *Humble yourselves therefore under the mighty hand of God, that he may exalt you in due time: Casting all your care upon him; for he careth for you. Be sober, be vigilant; because your adversary the devil, as a roaring lion, walketh about, seeking whom he may devour* **(I Peter 5:6-8)**.

By Jesus' stripes we are healed, and Satan's strifes are blocked by the Lord's shield.

God Wars

> *But he was wounded for our transgressions, he was bruised for our iniquities: the chastisement of our peace was upon him; and with his stripes we are healed* **(Isaiah 53:5)**. *He loveth transgression that loveth strife: and he that exalteth his gate seeketh destruction* **(Proverbs 17:19)**. *Above all, taking the shield of faith, wherewith ye shall be able to quench all the fiery darts of the wicked. And take the helmet of salvation, and the sword of the Spirit, which is the word of God* **(Ephesians 6:16-17)**.

Be led by the Holy Ghost, or be led by the devil to roast.

> *But the Comforter, which is the Holy Ghost, whom the Father will send in my name, he shall teach you all things, and bring all things to your remembrance, whatsoever I have said unto you **(John 14:26)**. Then was Jesus led up of the Spirit into the wilderness to be tempted of the devil **(Matthew 4:1)**. Then shall he say also unto them on the left hand, Depart from me, ye cursed, into everlasting fire, prepared for the devil and his angels **(Matthew 25:41)**.*

God is Jehovah Jireh! He's our guider; our number one provider. He gives us our hopes and desires, and the one to admire; as The Messiah.

> *And Abraham called the name of that place Je-ho'-vah-ji'-reh: as it is said to this day, In the mount of the LORD it shall be seen **(Genesis 22:14)**. But my God shall supply all your need according to his riches in glory by Christ Jesus **(Philippians 4:19)**. Be of good courage, and he shall strengthen your heart, all ye that hope in the LORD **(Psalm 31:24)**. Delight thyself also in the LORD: and he shall give thee the desires of thine heart **(Psalm 37:4)**. For God so loved the world, that he gave his only begotten Son, that whosoever believeth in him should not perish, but have everlasting life **(John 3:16)**.*

If you get angry and blow up,

you will allow a door to open for Satan to
show up.

*Be ye angry, and sin not: let not the sun go
down upon your wrath: Neither give place to
the devil **(Ephesians 4:26-27)**. Be not hasty
in thy spirit to be angry: for anger resteth in
the bosom of fools **(Ecclesiastes 7:9)**.*

When I put the enemy behind me, the Lord will start to shine me.

*But he turned, and said unto Peter, Get thee behind me, Satan: thou art an offence unto me: for thou savourest not the things that be of God, but those that be of men. Then said Jesus unto his disciples, If any man will come after me, let him deny himself, and take up his cross, and follow me **(Matthew 16:23-24)**. Let your light so shine before men, that they may see your good works, and glorify your Father which is in heaven **(Matthew 5:16)**.*

Be radical for Christ, because it was He who paid the price.

*For ye are bought with a price: therefore glorify God in your body, and in your spirit, which are God's **(I Corinthians 6:20)**. Looking unto Jesus the author and finisher of our faith; who for the joy that was set before him endured the cross, despising the shame, and is set down at the right hand of the throne of God **(Hebrews 12:2)**.*

When you allow the Holy Spirit to speak through you, that will allow others to see the true you.

Since ye seek a proof of Christ speaking in me, which to you-ward is not weak, but is mighty in you. For though he was crucified through weakness, yet he liveth by the power of God. For we also are weak in him, but we shall live with him by the power of God toward you **(II Corinthians 13:3-4)***. These are the things that ye shall do; Speak ye every man the truth to his neighbour; execute the judgment of truth and peace in your gates: And let none of you imagine evil in your hearts against his neighbour; and love no false oath: for all these are things that I hate, saith the* LORD **(Zechariah 8:16-17)**.

The enemy will try to hold you back, so stay intact with the Lord on His one accord, and He will take you forward.

While they promise them liberty, they themselves are the servants of corruption: for of whom a man is overcome, of the same is he brought in bondage **(II Peter 2:19)***. And deliver them who through fear of death were all their lifetime subject to bondage* **(Hebrews 2:15)***. Stand fast therefore in the liberty wherewith Christ hath made us free, and be not entangled again with the yoke of bondage* **(Galatians 5:1)**.

I hate every false way, and don't believe everything people say.

> *Therefore I esteem all thy precepts concerning all things to be right; and I hate every false way.* **(Psalm 119:128)**. *A false witness shall not be unpunished, and he that speaketh lies shall not escape* **(Proverbs 19:5)**. *Let the lying lips be put to silence; which speak grievous things proudly and contemptuously against the righteous* **(Psalm 31:18)**.

The Lord gives you power that will never run sour. He will baptize you in His shower, where you will grow as His Holy Glow flower that Satan cannot devour.

> *But they that wait upon the* LORD *shall renew their strength; they shall mount up with wings as eagles; they shall run, and not be weary; and they shall walk, and not faint* **(Isaiah 40:31)**. *And I will make them and the places round about my hill a blessing; and I will cause the shower to come down in his season; there shall be showers of blessing* **(Ezekiel 34:26)**. *Then remembered I the word of the Lord, how that he said, John indeed baptized with water; but ye shall be baptized with the Holy Ghost* **(Acts 11:16)**. *Be sober, be vigilant; because your adversary the devil, as a roaring lion, walketh about, seeking whom he may devour* **(I Peter 5:8)**.

The Lord answer's through His word, and through messages that's heard.

> *But he said, Yea rather, blessed are they that hear the word of God, and keep it* **(Luke 11:28)***. Wherefore lay apart all filthiness and superfluity of naughtiness, and receive with meekness the engrafted word, which is able to save your souls. But be ye doers of the word, and not hearers only, deceiving your own selves. For if any be a hearer of the word, and not a doer, he is like unto a man beholding his natural face in a glass: For he beholdeth himself, and goeth his way, and straightway forgetteth what manner of man he was* **(James 1:21-24)***. All scripture is given by inspiration of God, and is profitable for doctrine, for reproof, for correction, for instruction in righteousness: That the man of God may be perfect, thoroughly furnished unto all good works* **(II Timothy 3:16-17)***.*

The blood of Jesus is as the flood of Jesus.

> *For this is my blood of the new testament, which is shed for many for the remission of sins* **(Matthew 26:28)***.*

The Lord will never leave us nor forsake us, but it is the devil who will try to deceive and take us.

*Let your conversation be without covetousness; and be content with such things as ye have: for he hath said, I will never leave thee, nor forsake thee **(Hebrews 13:5)**. Be not deceived; God is not mocked: for whatsoever a man soweth, that shall he also reap. For he that soweth to his flesh shall of the flesh reap corruption; but he that soweth to the Spirit shall of the Spirit reap life everlasting **(Galatians 6:7-8)**.*

If you kill, you may lose your life deal. Not only will you serve jail time, but you may also serve hell time.

*Thou shalt not kill **(Exodus 20:13)**. Know ye not that the unrighteous shall not inherit the kingdom of God? Be not deceived: neither fornicators, nor idolaters, nor adulterers, nor effeminate, nor abusers of themselves with mankind, Nor thieves, nor covetous, nor drunkards, nor revilers, nor extortioners, shall inherit the kingdom of God. And such were some of you: but ye are washed, but ye are sanctified, but ye are justified in the name of the Lord Jesus, and by the Spirit of our God **(I Corinthians 6:9-11)**.*

As children, we had a curfew, but Satan is still on the loose, and gives us a curved-view.

Children, obey your parents in the Lord: for this is right. Honour thy father and mother; which is the first commandment with promise; That it may be well with thee, and thou mayest live long on the earth **(Ephesians 6:1-3)**. *Above all, taking the shield of faith, wherewith ye shall be able to quench all the fiery darts of the wicked. And take the helmet of salvation, and the sword of the Spirit, which is the word of God: Praying always with all prayer and supplication in the Spirit, and watching thereunto with all perseverance and supplication for all saints* **(Ephesians 6:16-18)**.

If you name it and claim it, in Jesus you can go all out and fame it.

And Jesus answering saith unto them, Have faith in God. For verily I say unto you, That whosoever shall say unto this mountain, Be thou removed, and be thou cast into the sea; and shall not doubt in his heart, but shall believe that those things which he saith shall come to pass; he shall have whatsoever he saith. Therefore I say unto you, What things soever ye desire, when ye pray, believe that ye receive them, and ye shall have them **(Mark 11:22-24)**.

Through the power of the Holy Spirit talking, is to strengthen other peoples walking.

> *He that hath an ear, let him hear what the Spirit saith unto the churches; To him that overcometh will I give to eat of the tree of life, which is in the midst of the paradise of God **(Revelation 2:7)**. Likewise the Spirit also helpeth our infirmities: for we know not what we should pray for as we ought: but the Spirit itself maketh intercession for us with groanings which cannot be uttered. And he that searcheth the hearts knoweth what is the mind of the Spirit, because he maketh intercession for the saints according to the will of God **(Romans 8:26-27)**.*

A blessing chaser is no praise eraser.

> *Not as though I had already attained, either were already perfect: but I follow after, if that I may apprehend that for which also I am apprehended of Christ Jesus. Brethren, I count not myself to have apprehended: but this one thing I do, forgetting those things which are behind, and reaching forth unto those things which are before, I press toward the mark for the prize of the high calling of God in Christ Jesus **(Philippians 3:12-14)**. By him therefore let us offer the sacrifice of praise to God continually, that is, the fruit of our lips giving thanks to his name **(Hebrews 13:15)**.*

No one can measure up to God's pleasure cup, because His cup runneth over and what we pour doesn't go beyond the cover.

> *The LORD is the portion of mine inheritance and of my cup: thou maintainest my lot* **(Psalm 16:5)**. *Thou prepares a table before me in presence of mine enemies: thou anointest my head with oil; my cup runneth over* **(Psalm 23:5)**. *How excellent is thy loving-kindness, O God! therefore the children of men put their trust under the shadow of thy wings. They shall be abundantly satisfied with the fatness of thy house; and thou shalt make them drink of the river of thy pleasures* **(Psalms 36:7-8)**.

You don't have to say it loud to say it proud. Keep up the silence to keep down the violence.

> *Wherefore, my beloved brethren, let every man be swift to hear, slow to speak, slow to wrath* **(James 1:19)**. *Even a fool, when he holdeth his peace, is counted wise: and he that shutteth his lips is esteemed a man of understanding* **(Proverbs 17:28)**. *But thou, when thou prayest, enter into thy closet, and when thou hast shut thy door, pray to thy Father which is in secret; and thy Father which seeth in secret shall reward thee openly* **(Matthew 6:6)**.

Fill your heart with praise,

because an empty place gives the devil space.

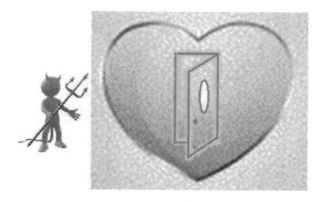

I will praise thee with my whole heart: before the gods will I sing praise unto thee. I will worship toward thy holy temple, and praise thy name for thy lovingkindness and for thy truth: for thou hast magnified thy word above all thy name. In the day when I cried thou answeredst

me, and strengthenedst me with strength in my soul. All the kings of the earth shall praise thee, O Lord, when they hear the words of thy mouth. Yea, they shall sing in the ways of the Lord: for great is the glory of the LORD **(Psalms 138:1-5)**. *Neither give place to the devil* **(Ephesians 4:27)**.

You have to have trust and not to fuss. That comes through lust. You have to have the spirit from God's lyrics.

Ye lust, and have not: ye kill, and desire to have, and cannot obtain: ye fight and war, yet ye have not, because ye ask not **(James 4:2)**. *Trust in the Lord with all thine heart; and lean not unto thine own understanding. In all thy ways acknowledge him, and he shall direct thy paths. Be not wise in thine own eyes: fear the Lord, and depart from evil. It shall be health to thy navel, and marrow to thy bones* **(Proverbs 3:5-8)**. *Teach me to do thy will; for thou art my God: thy spirit is good; lead me into the land of uprightness. Quicken me, O Lord, for thy name's sake: for thy righteousness' sake bring my soul out of trouble* **(Psalms 143:10-11)**. *This I say then, Walk in the Spirit, and ye shall not fulfil the lust of the flesh* **(Galatians 5:16)**.

God doesn't want you to be a worrier; He wants you to be a warrior.

Come unto me, all ye that labour and are heavy laden, and I will give you rest. Take my yoke upon you, and learn of me; for I am meek and lowly in heart: and ye shall find rest unto your souls. For my yoke is easy, and my burden is light **(Matthew 11:28-30)***. Casting all your care upon him; for he careth for you. Be sober, be vigilant; because your adversary the devil, as a roaring lion, walketh about, seeking whom he may devour***(1 Peter 5:7-8)***: Trust in the Lord with all thine heart; and lean not unto thine own understanding* **(Proverbs 3:5)***. Be careful for nothing; but in every thing by prayer and supplication with thanksgiving let your requests be made known unto God. And the peace of God, which passeth all understanding, shall keep your hearts and minds through Christ Jesus* **(Philippians 4:6-7)***.*

For the weapons of our warfare are not carnal, but mighty through God to the pulling down of strong holds **(2 Corinthians 10:4)***; Finally, my brethren, be strong in the Lord, and in the power of his might. Put on the whole armour of God, that ye may be able to stand against the wiles of the devil. For we wrestle not against flesh and blood, but against principalities, against powers, against the rulers of the darkness of this world, against spiritual wickedness in high places. Wherefore take unto you the whole armour of God, that ye*

*may be able to withstand in the evil day, and
having done all, to stand. Stand therefore, having
your loins girt about with truth, and having on the
breastplate of righteousness; And your feet shod
with the preparation of the gospel of peace; Above
all, taking the shield of faith, wherewith ye shall be
able to quench all the fiery darts of the wicked.
And take the helmet of salvation, and the sword of
the Spirit, which is the word of God: Praying
always with all prayer and supplication in the Spirit,
and watching thereunto with all perseverance and
supplication for all saints (Ephesians 6:10-18);*

The life is the fruit that will give you a
heavenly boost.

*Every branch in me that beareth not fruit
he taken away: and every branch that
beareth fruit, he purgeth it, that it may
bring forth more fruit (John 15:2).*

God does not create His men/women sorrow,
nor does He want us to be equipped to borrow.

*A merry heart maketh a cheerful countenance:
but by sorrow of the heart the spirit is broken
(Proverbs 15:13). For the LORD thy God
blesseth thee, as he promised thee: and thou
shalt lend unto many nations, but thou shalt not
borrow; and thou shalt reign over many nations,
but they shall not reign over thee
(Deuteronomy 15:6).*

The Lord, God is my King! He's my supply for everything.

But my God shall supply all your need according to his riches in glory by Christ Jesus **(Philippians 4:19)**. *For God is the King of all the earth: sing ye praises with understanding* **(Psalm 47:7)**.

CHAPTER 4

SERMON TITLES

"Let There Be No Delays In These Days We Give God Praise"

*I will bless the L*ORD *at all times: his praise shall continually be in my mouth. My soul shall make her boast in the L*ORD*: the humble shall hear thereof, and be glad. O magnify the L*ORD *with me, and let us exalt his name together* ***(Psalms 34:1-3)****. Because thy lovingkindness is better than life, my lips shall praise thee. Thus will I bless thee while I live: I will lift up my hands in thy name* ***(Psalms 63:3-4)****.*

"Be Grateful For Your Blessings, And Don't Dwell On Your Oppressions"

*The blessing of the LORD, it maketh rich, and he addeth no sorrow with it **(Proverbs 10:22)**.*

"Just Because You Don't Get Results Today, Don't Mean For You To Delay Your Pray"

*And he spake a parable unto them to this end, that men ought always to pray, and not to faint **(Luke 18:1)**. Pray without ceasing **(I Thessalonians 5:17)**.*

"Speak The Progression And Not The Problem"

*Keep thy tongue from evil, and thy lips from speaking guile. Depart from evil, and do good; seek peace, and pursue it **(Psalms 34:13-14)**.*

"Expect With No Reject"

*For surely there is an end; and thine expectation shall not be cut off **(Proverbs 23:18)**.*

"There Are Times Due For A Pray-Through In Order To Receive Your Breakthrough"

Pray without ceasing **(I Thessalonians 5:17)**.

"You Have To Forgive To Live"

And forgive us our debts, as we forgive our debtors. For if ye forgive men their trespasses, your heavenly Father will also forgive you: But if ye forgive not men their trespasses, neither will your Father forgive your trespasses. Moreover when ye fast, be not, as the hypocrites, of a sad countenance: for they disfigure their faces, that they may appear unto men to fast. Verily I say unto you, They have their reward **(Matthew 6:12, 14-16)**.   *And when ye stand praying, forgive, if ye have ought against any: that your Father also which is in heaven may forgive you your trespasses. But if ye do not forgive, neither will your Father which is in heaven forgive your trespasses* **(Mark 11:25-26)**.

"Keep Confessing Your Blessing Through The Power Of Your Tongue, And Know By Faith It's Already Done"

Death and life are in the power of the tongue: and they that love it shall eat the fruit thereof **(Proverbs 18:21)**.

"Your Attitude Determines Your Glad-itude/Gratitude"

Talk no more so exceeding proudly; let not arrogancy come out of your mouth: for the LORD is a God of knowledge, and by him actions are weighed **(1 Samuel 2:3)**. *One generation shall praise thy works to another, and shall declare thy mighty acts. I will speak of the glorious honour of thy majesty, and of thy wondrous works. And men shall speak of the might of thy terrible acts: and I will declare thy greatness. They shall abundantly utter the memory of thy great goodness, and shall sing of thy righteousness* **(Psalms 145:4-7)**. *Therefore my heart is glad, and my glory rejoiceth: my flesh also shall rest in hope. For thou wilt not leave my soul in hell; neither wilt thou suffer thine Holy One to see corruption. Thou wilt shew me the path of life: in thy presence is fullness of joy; at thy right hand there are pleasures for evermore* **(Psalm 9:11)**.

"Read The Word, And Have It Heard"

The Spirit of the Lord GOD is upon me; because the LORD hath anointed me to preach good tidings unto the meek; he hath sent me to bind up the brokenhearted, to proclaim liberty to the captives, and the opening of the prison to them that are bound **(Isaiah 61:1)**.

"Trust And Obey Him, Because Lust Don't Okay Him"

Teaching us that, denying ungodliness and worldly lusts, we should live soberly, righteously, and godly, in this present world **(Titus 2:12)**. *Whereby are given unto us exceeding great and precious promises: that by these ye might be partakers of the divine nature, having escaped the corruption that is in the world through lust* **(II Peter 1:4)**.

"We Have To Bind And Loose The Devil's Abuse"

*Can you bind the devil with
No strings attached?*

*The Spirit of the Lord GOD is upon me; because
the LORD hath anointed me to preach good
tidings unto the meek; he hath sent me to bind
up the brokenhearted, to proclaim liberty to the
captives, and the opening of the prison to them
that are bound (**Isaiah 61:1**). Verily I say
unto you, Whatsoever ye shall bind on earth
shall be bound in heaven: and whatsoever
ye shall loose on earth shall be loosed
in heaven (**Matthew 18:18**).*

"Patience Is A Virtue, If You Don't Have It, It May Hurt You"

And not only so, but we glory in tribulations also: knowing that tribulation worketh patience; And patience, experience; and experience, hope **(Romans 5:3-4)**.

"The Mode Of Receiving Is All Due To Believing"

Therefore I say unto you, What things soever ye desire, when ye pray, believe that ye receive them, and ye shall have them **(Mark 11:24)**.

"You Have To Go Through Enduring Before You Get To Ensuring"

Behold, we count them happy which endure. Ye have heard of the patience of Job, and have seen the end of the Lord; that the Lord is very pitiful, and of tender mercy **(James 5:11)**.

"Always Claim Hundredfold And Nothing Below"

Then Isaac sowed in that land, and received in The same year an hundredfold: and the LORD blessed him **(Genesis 26:12)**.

"Speak Those Things And Don't Weaken Those Things"

And Jesus answering saith unto them, Have faith in God. For verily I say unto you, That whosoever shall say unto this mountain, Be thou removed, and be thou cast into the sea; and shall not doubt in his heart, but shall believe that those things which he saith shall come to pass; he shall have whatsoever he saith. Therefore I say unto you, What things soever ye desire, when ye pray, believe that ye receive them, and ye shall have them **(Mark 11:22-24)**.

"It's Never Too Late To Participate"

Dare any of you, having a matter against another, go to law before the unjust, and not before the saints **(I Corinthians 6:17)**. *Let your conversation be without covetousness; and be content with such things as ye have: for he hath said, I will never leave thee, nor forsake thee* **(Hebrews 13:5)**. *They shall ask the way to Zion with their faces thitherward, saying, Come, and let us join ourselves to the* LORD *in a perpetual covenant that shall not be forgotten* **(Jeremiah 50:5)**.

"We Have To Guard Our Minds To Stay In Line"

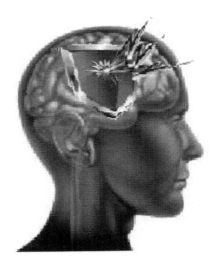

Thou wilt keep him in perfect peace, whose mind is stayed on thee: because he trusteth in thee. Trust ye in the LORD for ever: for in the LORD JEHOVAH is everlasting strength **(Isaiah 26:3-4)**.

"The Lord's Mercy Over Powers Satan Intentions Of Cursing Me"

Be merciful unto me, O God: for man would swallow me up; he fighting daily oppresseth me. Mine enemies would daily swallow me up: for they be many that fight against me, O thou most High **(Psalms 56:1-2)**. *Surely goodness and mercy shall follow me all the days of my life: and I will dwell in the house of the LORD for ever* **(Psalm 23:6)**.

"Join The Lord's Track, So You Can Win The Race For Victory"

*They shall ask the way to Zion with their faces thitherward, saying, Come, and let us join ourselves to the LORD in a perpetual covenant that shall not be forgotten **(Jeremiah 50:5)**.*

"My Past Is My Plus When I'm Doing Just"

*And we know that all things work together for good to them that love God, to them who are the called according to his purpose **(Romans 8:28)**. The way of the just is uprightness: thou, most upright, dost weigh the path of the just **(Isaiah 26:7)**.*

"We Have To Praise God, Until We Amaze God"

I will bless the LORD *at all times: his praise shall continually be in my mouth **(Psalm 34:1)**. By him therefore let us offer the sacrifice of praise to God continually, that is, the fruit of our lips giving thanks to his name **(Hebrews 13:15)**.*

"Stay Uplifted In Christ, And Never Be Shifted From Christ"

But they that wait upon the LORD *shall renew their strength; they shall mount up with wings as eagles; they shall run, and not be weary; and they shall walk, and not faint **(Isaiah 40:31)**. For I am persuaded, that neither death, nor life, nor angels, nor principalities, nor powers, nor things present, nor things to come, Nor height, nor depth, nor any other creature, shall be able to separate us from the love of God, which is in Christ Jesus our Lord **(Romans 8:38-39)**.*

"Do A Praise Shabach And Present It To The Rock"

Praise Shabach

O come, let us sing unto the LORD: let us make a joyful noise to the rock of our salvation. Let us come before his presence with thanksgiving, and make a joyful noise unto him with psalms. For the LORD is a great God, and a great King above all gods **(Psalms 95:1-3)**.

"When People Offer You Their Hurts, The Lord Can Turn It Around For Your Worth"

But as for you, ye thought evil against me; but God meant it unto good, to bring to pass, as it is this day, to save much people alive **(Genesis 50:20)**.

273

"The Lord Will Bring Confirmation Through Conversation"

How shall we escape, if we neglect so great salvation; which at the first began to be spoken by the Lord, and was confirmed unto us by them that heard him; God also bearing them witness, both with signs and wonders, and with divers miracles, and gifts of the Holy Ghost, according to his own will (Hebrews 2:3-4). Even as the testimony of Christ was confirmed in you: So that ye come behind in no gift; waiting for the coming of our Lord Jesus Christ: Who shall also confirm you unto the end, that ye may be blameless in the day of our Lord Jesus Christ (I Corinthians 1:6-8). And they went forth, and preached every where, the Lord working with them, and confirming the word with signs following. Amen (Mark 16:20).

"Don't Race The Course, Let God Handle Your Force"

Remember ye not the former things, neither consider the things of old. Behold, I will do a new thing; now it shall spring forth; shall ye not know it? I will even make a way in the wilderness, and rivers in the desert (Isaiah 43:18-19). Trust in the LORD with all thine heart; and lean not unto thine own understanding. In all thy ways acknowledge him, and he shall direct thy paths (Proverbs 3:5-6).

"God's Got Me Covered Where No Other Can Discover"

*The God of my rock; in him will I trust: he is my shield, and the horn of my salvation, my high tower, and my refuge, my saviour; thou savest me from violence. I will all on the LORD, who is worthy to be praised: so shall I be saved from mine enemies **(II Samuel 22:3–4)**. I will both lay me down in peace, and sleep: for thou, LORD, only makest me dwell in safety **(Psalm 4:8)**. As for God, his way is perfect: the word of the LORD is tried: he is a buckler to all those that trust in him **(Psalm 18:30)**. Thou shalt hide them in the secret of thy presence from the pride of man: thou shalt keep them secretly in a pavilion from the strife of tongues **(Psalm 31:20)**. Thou art my hiding place; thou shalt preserve me from trouble; thou shalt compass me about with songs of deliverance. Selah **(Psalm 32:7)**. How excellent is thy lovingkindness, O God! therefore the children of men put their trust under the shadow of thy wings **(Psalm 36:7)**.*

"What The Lord Sent Was For Your Hint"

A message from the Lord is a massage of wisdom from His word.

*God also bearing them witness, both with signs and wonders, and with divers miracles, and gifts of the Holy Ghost, according to his own will **(Hebrews 2:4)**. And they went forth, and preached every where, the Lord working with them, and confirming the word with signs following. Amen **(Mark 16:20)**.*

"Confirmation Of God's Information"

Therefore we ought to give the more earnest heed to the things which we have heard, lest at any time we should let them slip. For if the word spoken by angels was stedfast, and every transgression and disobedience received a just recompence of reward; How shall we escape, if we neglect so great salvation; which at the first began to be spoken by the Lord, and was confirmed unto us by them that heard him; God also bearing them witness, both with signs and wonders, and with divers miracles, and gifts of the Holy Ghost, according to his own will **(Hebrews 2:1-4)**. *And he said unto them, Go ye into all the world, and preach the gospel to every creature. He that believeth and is baptized shall be saved; but he that believeth not shall be damned.   And these signs shall follow them that believe; In my name shall they cast out devils; they shall speak with new tongues; They shall take up serpents; and if they drink any deadly thing, it shall not hurt them; they shall lay hands on the sick, and they shall recover. So then after the Lord had spoken unto them, he was received up into heaven, and sat on the right hand of God. And they went forth, and preached every where, the Lord working with them, and confirming the word with signs following. Amen* **(Mark 16:15-20)**.

"God's Master Plan Is Always In Demand"

God's plan still stands. It's a onefold in one roll.

*For the word of the LORD is right; and all his works are done in truth. He loveth righteousness and judgment: the earth is full of the goodness of the LORD. By the word of the LORD were the heavens made; and all the host of them by the breath of his mouth. He gathereth the waters of the sea together as an heap: he layeth up the depth in storehouses. Let all the earth fear the LORD: let all the inhabitants of the world stand in awe of him. For he spake, and it was done; he commanded, and it stood fast. The LORD bringeth the counsel of the heathen to nought: he maketh the devices of the people of none effect. The counsel of the LORD standeth for ever, the thoughts of his heart to all generations. Blessed is the nation whose God is the LORD; and the people whom he hath chosen for his own inheritance. The LORD looketh from heaven; he beholdeth all the sons of men. From the place of his habitation he looketh upon all the inhabitants of the earth **(Psalms 33:4-14)**.*

"Believe In The Father Of Trust, And Not In Man Of Flesh"

*It is better to trust in the L*ORD *than to put confidence in man (**Psalm 118:8**). I will say of the L*ORD*, He is my refuge and my fortress: my God; in him will I trust (**Psalm 91:2**). Trust in the L*ORD *with all thine heart; and lean not unto thine own understanding (**Proverbs 3:5**). Be sober, be vigilant; because your adversary the devil, as a roaring lion, walketh about, seeking whom he may devour (**I Peter 5:8**). Lest Satan should get an advantage of us: for we are not ignorant of his devices (**II Corinthians 2:11**). Submit yourselves therefore to God. Resist the devil, and he will flee from you (**James 4:7**). Ye are of God, little children, and have overcome them: because greater is he that is in you, than he that is in the world (**I John 4:4**).*

"You Have To Do It By Faith To Go Through It God's Way"

*For we walk by faith, not by sight: We are confident, I say, and willing rather to be absent from the body, and to be present with the Lord (**II Corinthians 5:7-8**).*

"Negative Feedback Can Hold Your Deed Back"

*O israel, return unto the LORD thy God; for thou hast fallen by thine iniquity. Take with you words, and turn to the LORD: say unto him, Take away all iniquity, and receive us graciously: so will we render the calves of our lips **(Hosea 14:1-2)**. Finally, my brethren, be strong in the Lord, and in the power of his might. Put on the whole armour of God, that ye may be able to stand against the wiles of the devil. For we wrestle not against flesh and blood, but against principalities, against powers, against the rulers of the darkness of this world, against spiritual wickedness in high places **(Ephesians 6:10-12)**.*

"You Have To Feel The Strange Before You Get To The Change"

*I have written to him the great things of my law, but they were counted as a strange thing **(Hosea 8:12)**. Beloved, think it not strange concerning the fiery trial which is to try you, as though some strange thing happened unto you: But rejoice, inasmuch as ye are partakers of Christ's sufferings; that, when his glory shall be revealed, ye may be glad also with exceeding joy **(I Peter 4:12-13)**. For I know the thoughts that I think toward you, saith the LORD, thoughts of peace, and not of evil, to give you an expected end **(Jeremiah 29:11)**.*

"Experience God's Motion, Take A Dip Into His Ocean"

Taking a dip in God's ocean will qualify you for divine promotion.

*And now why tarriest thou? arise, and be baptized, and wash away thy sins, calling on the name of the Lord **(Acts 22:16)**. Wash me throughly from mine iniquity, and cleanse me from my sin **(Psalm 51:2)**.*

"Going From Poverty To Prosperity"

*But of the children of Israel did Solomon make no servants for his work; but they were men of war, and chief of his captains, and captains of his chariots and horsemen **(II Chronicles 8:9)**. The blessing of the LORD, it maketh rich, and he addeth no sorrow with it **(Proverbs 10:22)**.*

"When God Put A Date On It, Don't Procrastinate On It"

*The soul of the sluggard desireth, and hath nothing: but the soul of the diligent shall be made fat **(Proverbs 13:4)**. The way of the slothful man is as an hedge of thorns: but the way of the righteous is made plain **(Proverbs 15:19)**.*

"The Blood Of Jesus Speaks Volumes"

*And almost all things are by the law purged with blood; and without shedding of blood is no remission **(Hebrews 9:22)**. For this is my blood of the new testament, which is shed for many for the remission of sins **(Matthew 26:28)**. And they sung a new song, saying, Thou art worthy to take the book, and to open the seals thereof: for thou wast slain, and hast redeemed us to God by thy blood out of every kindred, and tongue, and people, and nation **(Revelation 5:9)**.*

"If We Don't Stay On Track, We Can Get Smacked By The Devil's Attack"

*If you don't know which track to go,
ask God, and He will tell you so.*

Finally, my brethren, be strong in the Lord, and in the power of his might. Put on the whole armour of God, that ye may be able to stand against the wiles of the devil. For we wrestle not against flesh and blood, but against principalities, against powers, against the rulers of the darkness of this world, against spiritual wickedness in high places. Wherefore take unto you the whole armour of God, that ye may be able to withstand in the evil day, and having done all, to stand. Stand therefore, having your loins girt about with truth, and having on the breastplate of righteousness; And your feet shod with the preparation of the gospel of peace; Above all, taking the shield of faith, wherewith ye shall be able to quench all the fiery darts of the wicked. And take the helmet of salvation, and the sword of the Spirit, which is the word of God **(Ephesians 6:10-17)**. *Submit yourselves therefore to God. Resist the devil, and he will flee from you* **(James 4:7)**.

"Go From Uptight To Upright"

*He that is soon angry dealeth foolishly: and a man of wicked devices is hated. The simple inherit folly: but the prudent are crowned with knowledge. The evil bow before the good; and the wicked at the gates of the righteous **(Proverbs 14:17–19)**. I am the LORD your God, which brought you forth out of the land of Egypt, that ye should not be their bondmen; and I have broken the bands of your yoke, and made you go upright **(Leviticus 26:13)**.*

"A Humble Beginning, No Losing, All Winning"

*And it came to pass, as he went into the house of one of the chief Pharisees to eat bread on the sabbath day, that they watched him **(Luke 14:1)**. Humble yourselves therefore under the mighty hand of God, that he may exalt you in due time **(I Peter 5:6)**. What shall we then say to these things? If God be for us, who can be against us **(Romans 8:31)**?*

"If Your Soul Is Out To God, Then You Are Sold Out For God"

*And thou shalt love the LORD thy God with all thine heart, and with all thy soul, and with all thy might **(Deuteronomy 6:5)**. For ye are bought with a price: therefore glorify God in your body, and in your spirit, which are God's **(I Corinthians 6:20)**.*

"Would You Rather Live For Etern, Or Would You Rather Burn?"

"Living For Eternity"   or   *"Burning For Hell"*

He that believeth on the Son of God hath the witness in himself: he that believeth not God hath made him a liar; because he believeth not the record that God gave of his Son. And this is the record, that God hath given to us eternal life, and this life is in his Son. He that hath the Son hath life; [and] he that hath not the Son of God hath not life. These things have I written unto you that believe on the name of the Son of God; that ye may know that ye have eternal life, and that ye may believe on the name of the Son of God **(I John 5:10-13)**. *And the beast was taken, and with him the false prophet that wrought miracles before him, with which he deceived them that had received the mark of the beast, and them that worshipped his image. These both were cast alive into a lake of fire burning with brimstone* **(Revelation 19:20)**.

"God Wants Us To Be Legit, And Have The Faith To Never Quit"

*Beloved, believe not every spirit, but try the spirits whether they are of God: because many false prophets are gone out into the world **(I John 4:1)**. And let none of you imagine evil in your hearts against his neighbour; and love no false oath: for all these are things that I hate, saith the* LORD ***(Zechariah 8:17)***.
*Blessed are ye, when men shall revile you, and persecute you, and shall say all manner of evil against you falsely, for my sake. Rejoice, and be exceeding glad: for great is your reward in heaven: for so persecuted they the prophets which were before you **(Matthew 5:11-12)**. He giveth power to the faint; and to them that have no might he increaseth strength. Even the youths shall faint and be weary, and the young men shall utterly fall: But they that wait upon the* LORD *shall renew their strength; they shall mount up with wings as eagles; they shall run, and not be weary; and they shall walk, and not faint **(Isaiah 40:29-31)**.*

"God's Not Here To Hurt You, He's Here To Work With You"

*For I know the thoughts that I think toward you, saith the LORD, thoughts of peace, and not of evil, to give you an expected end **(Jeremiah 29:11)**.*

"Total Recovery Is God's Discovery"

And a woman having an issue of blood twelve years, which had spent all her living upon physicians, neither could be healed of any, Came behind him, and touched the border of his garment: and immediately her issue of blood stanched. And Jesus said, Who touched me? When all denied, Peter and they that were with him said, Master, the multitude throng thee and press thee, and sayest thou, Who touched me? And Jesus said, Somebody hath touched me: for I perceive that virtue is gone out of me. And when the woman saw that she was not hid, she came trembling, and falling down before him, she declared unto him before all the people for what cause she had touched him, and how she was healed immediately. And he said unto her, Daughter, be of good comfort: thy faith hath made thee whole; go in peace **(Luke 8:43-48)**. *But Jesus beheld them, and said unto them, With men this is impossible; but with God all things are possible* **(Matthew 19:26)**.

"Don't Let Your Negative Visions Control Your Decisions"

There are many devices in a man's heart; nevertheless the counsel of the LORD, that shall stand **(Proverbs 19:21)**. *A man heart deviseth his way: but the LORD directeth his steps* **(Proverbs 16:9)**.

"If You Seek God, You Will See God"

Ho, every one that thirsteth, come ye to the waters, and he that hath no money; come ye, buy, and eat; yea, come, buy wine and milk without money and without price. Wherefore do ye spend money for that which is not bread? And your labour for that which satisfieth not? hearken diligently unto me, and eat ye that which is good, and let your soul delight itself in fatness. Incline your ear, and come unto me: hear, and your soul shall live; and I will make an everlasting covenant with you, even the sure mercies of David. Behold, I have given him for a witness to the people, a leader and commander to the people. Behold, thou shalt call a nation that thou knowest not, and nations that knew not thee shall run unto thee because of the LORD thy God, and for the Holy One of Israel; for he hath glorified thee. Seek ye the LORD while he may be found, call ye upon him while he is near **(Isaiah 55:1-6)**.

"Faith Causes Your Praise To Rise, And Goes Beyond The Skies"

*Now faith is the substance of things hoped for, the evidence of things not seen **(Hebrews 11:1)**. But without faith it is impossible to please him: for he that cometh to God must believe that he is, and that he is a rewarder of them that diligently seek him **(Hebrews 11:6)**. Rejoice in the LORD, O ye righteous: for praise is comely for the upright. Praise the LORD with harp: sing unto him with the psaltery and an instrument of ten strings. Sing unto him a new song; play skilfully with a loud noise. For the word of the LORD is right; and all his works are done in truth **(Psalms 33:1-4)**. I will sing unto the LORD as long as I live: I will sing praise to my God while I have my being **(Psalm 104:33)**. By him therefore let us offer the sacrifice of praise to God continually, that is, the fruit of our lips giving thanks to his name **(Hebrews 13:15)**.*

"Christ In You Is The Price In You"

*For ye are bought with a price: therefore glorify God in your body, and in your spirit, which are God's **(I Corinthians 6:20)**. But ye are a chosen generation, a royal priesthood, an holy nation, a peculiar people; that ye should shew forth the praises of him who hath called you out of darkness into his marvellous light **(I Peter 2:9)**.*

"It's Time To Get Set To Be Blessed"

Now there was a day when the sons of God came to present themselves before the LORD, and Satan came also among them. And the LORD said unto Satan, Whence comest thou? Then Satan answered the LORD, and said, From going to and fro in the earth, and from walking up and down in it. And the LORD said unto Satan, Hast thou considered my servant Job, that there is none like him in the earth, a perfect and an upright man, one that feareth God, and escheweth evil? Then Satan answered the LORD, and said, Doth Job fear God for nought? Hast not thou made an hedge about him, and about his house, and about all that he hath on every side? thou hast blessed the work of his hands, and his substance is increased in the land. But put forth thine hand now, and touch all that he hath, and he will curse thee to thy face. And the LORD said unto Satan, Behold, all that he hath is in thy power; only upon himself put not forth thine hand. So Satan went forth from the presence of the LORD. And there was a day when his sons and his daughters were eating and drinking wine in their eldest brother's house: And there came a messenger unto Job, and said, The oxen were plowing, and the asses feeding beside them: And the Sabeans fell upon them, and took them away; yea, they have slain the servants with the edge of the sword; and I only am escaped alone to tell thee. While he was yet speaking, there came also another, and said,

*The fire of God is fallen from heaven, and hath burned up the sheep, and the servants, and consumed them; and I only am escaped alone to tell thee. While he was yet speaking, there came also another, and said, The Chal-de'-ans made out three bands, and fell upon the camels, and have carried them away, yea, and slain the servants with the edge of the sword; and I only am escaped alone to tell thee. While he was yet speaking, there came also another, and said, Thy sons and thy daughters were eating and drinking wine in their eldest brother's house: And, behold, there came a great wind from the wilderness, and smote the four corners of the house, and it fell upon the young men, and they are dead; and I only am escaped alone to tell thee **(Job 1:6-19)**. Then Job arose, and rent his mantle, and shaved his head, and fell down upon the ground, and worshipped, And said, Naked came I out of my mother's womb, and naked shall I return thither: the LORD gave, and the LORD hath taken away; blessed be the name of the LORD. In all this Job sinned not, nor charged God foolishly **(Job 1:20-22)**. And the LORD turned the captivity of Job, when he prayed for his friends: also the LORD gave Job twice as much as he had before **(Job 42:10)**.*

"No More Doubting, Only Holy Ghost Shouting"

*I will therefore that men pray every where, lifting up holy hands, without wrath and doubting **(I Timothy 2:8)**.*

"The Lord's Not Finished Yet, Through All His Time And Sweat"

*Behold ye among the heathen, and regard, and wonder marvelously: for I will work a work in your days which ye will not believe, though it be told you **(Habakkuk 1:5)**. I must work the works of him that sent me, while it is day: the night cometh, when no man can work. As long as I am in the world, I am the light of the world **(John 9:4-5)**.*

"Why Make Life Foul? We're Only Here For A Little While!"

This I say therefore, and testify in the Lord, that ye henceforth walk not as other Gentiles walk, in the vanity of their mind, Having the understanding darkened, being alienated from the life of God through the ignorance that is in them, because of the blindness of their heart: Who being past feeling have given themselves over unto lasciviousness, to work all uncleanness with greediness. But ye have not so learned Christ; If so be that ye have heard him, and have been taught by him, as the truth is in Jesus: That ye put off concerning the former conversation the old man, which is corrupt according to the deceitful lusts **(Ephesians 4:17-22)**. *Let no man deceive you with vain words: for because of these things cometh the wrath of God upon the children of disobedience. Be not ye therefore partakers with them. For ye were sometimes darkness, but now are ye light in the Lord: walk as children of light* **(Ephesians 5:6-8)**. *For when they speak great swelling words of vanity, they allure through the lusts of the flesh, through much wantonness, those that were clean escaped from them who live in error. While they promise them liberty, they themselves are the servants of corruption: for of whom a man is overcome, of the same is he brought in bondage. For if after they have escaped the pollutions of the world through the knowledge* of the Lord and Saviour Jesus Christ, they are again entangled therein, and overcome, the latter end is worse with them than the beginning. For it had been better for them not to have known the way of righteousness, than, after they have known it, to turn from the holy commandment delivered unto them. But it is happened unto them according to the true proverb, The dog is turned to his own vomit again; and the sow that was washed to her wallowing in the mire **(II Peter 2:18-22)**. For yet a little while, and he that shall come will come, and will not tarry **(Hebrews 10:37)**.

"If You Have The Faith To Do It, The Lord Will Help You Through It"

And Jesus said unto them, Because of your unbelief: for verily I say unto you, If ye have faith as a grain of mustard seed, ye shall say unto this mountain, Remove hence to yonder place; and it shall remove; and nothing shall be impossible unto you. Howbeit this kind goeth not out but by prayer and fasting **(Matthew 17:20-21)**. For therein is the righteousness of God revealed from faith to faith: as it is written, The just shall live by faith **(Romans 1:17)**.

"Form A Line For Jesus Wine"

And he took the cup, and gave thanks, and gave it to them, saying, Drink ye all of it; For this is my blood of the new testament, which is shed for many for the remission of sins. But I say unto you, I will not drink henceforth of this fruit of the vine, until that day when I drink it new with you in my Father's kingdom **(Matthew 26:27-29)**.

"The Humble Don't Grumble"

Do all things without murmurings and disputings **(Philippians 2:14)**. *Better it is to be of an humble spirit with the lowly, than to divide the spoil with the proud* **(Proverbs 16:19)**. *Humble yourselves therefore under the mighty hand of God, that he may exalt you in due time* **(I Peter 5:6)**.

295

"Whatever You Speak Will Qualify Your Reach"

When you reach for God's Headquarters, your life won't be shorter.

And Jesus answering saith unto them, Have faith in God. *For verily I say unto you, That whosoever shall say unto this mountain, Be thou removed, and be thou cast into the sea; and shall not doubt in his heart, but shall believe that those things which he saith shall come to pass; he shall have whatsoever he saith. Therefore I say unto you, What things soever ye desire, when ye pray, believe that ye receive them, and ye shall have them* **(Mark 11:22-24)**. *Death and life are in the power of the tongue: and they that love it shall eat the fruit thereof* **(Proverbs 18:21)**. *And all things, whatsoever ye shall ask in prayer, believing, ye shall receive* **(Matthew 21:22)**.

"You Can't Be Founded, Unless You Were Grounded"

*It's good to be planted in
God's word.*

*That Christ may dwell in your hearts by faith;
that ye, being rooted and grounded in love
(Ephesians 3:17). Wherefore, beloved,
seeing that ye look for such things, be diligent
that ye may be found of him in peace, without
spot, and blameless **(II Peter 3:14)**. As ye
have therefore received Christ Jesus the Lord,
so walk ye in him: Rooted and built up in him,
and stablished in the faith, as ye have been
taught, abounding therein with thanksgiving
(Colossians 2:6-7).*

"Put Your Belief In The Cornerstone Chief"

*And are built upon the foundation of the
apostles and prophets, Jesus Christ himself
being the chief corner stone
(Ephesians 2:20).*

"Jesus Is Not Only Christ, But He Also Paid The Price"

For ye are bought with a price: therefore glorify God in your body, and in your spirit, which are God's **(I Corinthians 6:20).**

"God's Food Should Go To Taste And Never Go To Waste"

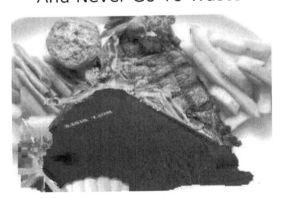

God's word is at stake/steak.

How sweet are thy words unto my taste! yea, sweeter than honey to my mouth! Through thy precepts I get understanding: therefore I hate every false way **(Psalms 119:103-104).**

"Temptation Will Violate God's Rules Of Dedication"

*But they that will be rich fall into temptation and a snare, and into many foolish and hurtful lusts, which drown men in destruction and perdition **(I Timothy 6:9)**. Brethren, if a man be overtaken in a fault, ye which are spiritual, restore such an one in the spirit of meekness; considering thyself, lest thou also be tempted **(Galatians 6:1)**. Blessed is the man that endureth temptation: for when he is tried, he shall receive the crown of life, which the Lord hath promised to them that love him. Let no man say when he is tempted, I am tempted of God: for God cannot be tempted with evil, neither tempteth he any man: But every man is tempted, when he is drawn away of his own lust, and enticed. Then when lust hath conceived, it bringeth forth sin: and sin, when it is finished, bringeth forth death. Do not err, my beloved brethren **(James 1:12-16)**.*

"What's To Come Is To Look What's Beyond"

*Remember ye not the former things, neither consider the things of old. Behold, I will do a new thing; now it shall spring forth; shall ye not know it? I will even make a way in the wilderness, and rivers in the desert **(Isaiah 43:18-19)**.*

"Don't Rush The Days, Enjoy The Praise"

*Make a joyful noise unto God, all ye lands: Sing forth the honour of his name: make his praise glorious **(Psalms 66:1-2)**. I will sing unto the LORD as long as I live: I will sing praise to my God while I have my being. My meditation of him shall be sweet: I will be glad in the LORD **(Psalms 104:33-34)**. Because thy lovingkindness is better than life, my lips shall praise thee. Thus will I bless thee while I live: I will lift up my hands in thy name **(Psalms 63:3-4)**.*

"Represent The One God Sent"

*Herein is love, not that we loved God, but that he loved us, and sent his Son to be the propitiation for our sins **(I John 4:10)**. And when he had so said, he shewed unto them his hands and his side. Then were the disciples glad, when they saw the* LORD. *Then said Jesus to them again, Peace be unto you: as my Father hath sent me, even so send I you **(John 20:20-21)**. Then spake Jesus again unto them, saying, I am the light of the world: he that followeth me shall not walk in darkness, but shall have the light of life **(John 8:12)**. But if we walk in the light, as he is in the light, we have fellowship one with another, and the blood of Jesus Christ his Son cleanseth us from all sin **(I John 1:7)**. But we all, with open face beholding as in a glass the glory of the Lord, are changed into the same image from glory to glory, even as by the Spirit of the Lord **(II Corinthians 3:18)**.*

"Don't Fight When People Don't Treat You Right"

If ye then be risen with Christ, seek those things which are above, where Christ sitteth on the right hand of God. Set your affection on things above, not on things on the earth. For ye are dead, and your life is hid with Christ in God. When Christ, who is our life, shall appear, then shall ye also appear with him in glory **(Colossians 3:1-4)**. *There is therefore now no condemnation to them which are in Christ Jesus, who walk not after the flesh, but after the Spirit. For the law of the Spirit of life in Christ Jesus hath made me free from the law of sin and death. For what the law could not do, in that it was weak through the flesh, God sending his own Son in the likeness of sinful flesh, and for sin, condemned sin in the flesh: That the righteousness of the law might be fulfilled in us, who walk not after the flesh, but after the Spirit* **(Romans 8:1-4)**. *A man's heart deviseth his way: but the* LORD *directeth his steps. A divine sentence is in the lips of the king: his mouth transgresseth not in judgment* **(Proverbs 16:9-10)**.

"You Will Reap A Bad Reflect From Bad Respect"

Be not deceived; God is not mocked: for whatsoever a man soweth, that shall he also reap **(Galatians 6:7)**.

"Jesus Paid It All, So We Wouldn't Have To Fall"

*But God commendeth his love toward us, in that, while we were yet sinners, Christ died for us **(Romans 5:8)**. And you, being dead in your sins and the uncircumcision of your flesh, hath he quickened together with him, having forgiven you all trespasses; Blotting out the handwriting of ordinances that was against us, which was contrary to us, and took it out of the way, nailing it to his cross **(Colossians 2:13-14)**. Now unto him that is able to keep you from falling, and to present you faultless before the presence of his glory with exceeding joy, To the only wise God our Saviour, be glory and majesty, dominion and power, both now and ever. Amen **(Jude 1:24-25)**.*

"We Didn't Pay The Cost, Jesus Bared The Cross"

*Hereby perceive we the love of God, because he laid down his life for us: and we ought to lay down our lives for the brethren **(I John 3:16)**. And, having made peace through the blood of his cross, by him to reconcile all things unto himself; by him, I say, whether they be things in earth, or things in heaven **(Colossians 1:20)**. And he is the propitiation for our sins: and not for ours only, but also for the sins of the whole world **(I John 2:2)**.*

"The Bible Is Your Survival"

When we are in the salvation of the army in the presence of the Lord, and planted in His word, He will raise us up to higher realms in the spirit of His word when we come together as one army to pray.

As newborn babes, desire the sincere milk of the word, that ye may grow thereby: If so be ye have tasted that the Lord is gracious **(I Peter 2:2-3)**. *For the word of God is quick, and powerful, and sharper than any twoedged sword, piercing even to the dividing asunder of soul and spirit, and of the joints and marrow, and is a discerner of the thoughts and intents of the heart* **(Hebrews 4:12)**.

"Raise Them To Praise Him"
In other words: Give your hands
a raise to give Jesus praise.

*And I, if I be lifted up from the earth, will draw all men unto me **(John 12:32)**. Thou art worthy, O Lord, to receive glory and honour and power: for thou hast created all things, and for thy pleasure they are and were created **(Revelation 4:11)**.*

"The Lord's Move In Your Life Takes Place Between Your Obedience And Strife"

*And Samuel said, Hath the LORD as great delight in burnt offerings and sacrifices, as in obeying the voice of the LORD? Behold, to obey is better than sacrifice, and to hearken than the fat of rams **(I Samuel 15:22)**. Whosoever therefore resisteth the power, resisteth the ordinance of God: and they that resist shall receive to themselves damnation **(Romans 13:2)**.*

"You Have To Fear Him To Hear Him"

Come and hear, all ye that fear God, and I will declare what he hath done for my soul **(Psalm 66:16)**. *"You Can't Erase What The Lord Promised You Through Grace" But God, who is rich in mercy, for his great love wherewith he loved us, Even when we were dead in sins, hath quickened us together with Christ, (by grace ye are saved;) And hath raised us up together, and made us sit together in heavenly places in Christ Jesus: That in the ages to come he might shew the exceeding riches of his grace in his kindness toward us through Christ Jesus. For by grace are ye saved through faith; and that not of yourselves: it is the gift of God* **(Ephesians 2:4-8)**. *In hope of eternal life, which God, that cannot lie, promised before the world began* **(Titus 1:2)**.

"Being Anxious Brings Confusion, But Patience Is The Solution"

Be careful for nothing; but in every thing by prayer and supplication with thanksgiving let your requests be made known unto God. And the peace of God, which passeth all understanding, shell keep your hearts and minds through Christ Jesus **(Philippians 4:6-7)**. *Casting all your care upon him; for he careth for you* **(1 Peter 5:7)**.

"Your Enemies Can Try To Detain You, But They Can't Chain You"

I will never forget thy precepts: for with them thou hast quickened me. I am thine, save me: for I have sought thy precepts. The wicked have waited for me; for me to destroy me: but I will consider thy testimonies. I have seen an end of all perfection: but thy commandment is exceeding broad. O how love I thy law! it is my meditation all the day. Thou through thy commandments hast made me wiser than mine enemies: for they are ever with me. I have more understanding than all my teachers: for thy testimonies are my meditation. I understand more than the ancients, because I keep thy precepts. I have refrained my feet from every evil way, that I might keep thy word. I have not departed from thy judgments: for thou hast taught me. How sweet are thy words unto my taste! yea, sweeter than honey to my mouth. Through thy precepts I get understanding: therefore I hate every false way **(Psalms 119:93-104)**.

"Be Honest, And Don't Be A Con-nist"

*Providing for honest things, not only in the sight of the Lord, but also in the sight of men **(2 Corinthians 8:21)**. He that walketh uprightly walketh surely: but he that perverteth his ways shall be known **(Proverbs 10:9)**.*

"There's A Special 'What To Say' When You Don't Know What To Pray"

*Likewise the Spirit also helpeth our infirmities: for we know not what we should pray for as we ought: but the Spirit itself maketh intercession for us with groanings which cannot be uttered. And he that searcheth the hearts knoweth what is the mind of the Spirit, because he maketh intercession for the saints according to the will of God **(Romans 8:26-27)**. And it came to pass, that, as he was praying in a certain place, when he ceased, one of his disciples said unto him, Lord, teach us to pray, as John also taught his disciples. And he said unto them, When ye pray, say, Our Father which art in heaven, Hallowed be thy name. Thy kingdom come. Thy will be done, as in heaven, so in earth. Give us day by day our daily bread. And forgive us our sins; for we also forgive every one that is indebted to us. And lead us not into temptation; but deliver us from evil **(Luke 11:1-4)**.*

"Stop The Press And Get Some Rest"

Rest in the LORD, and wait patiently for him: fret not thyself because of him who prospereth in his way, because of the man who bringeth wicked devices to pass **(Psalm 37:7)**. *Come unto me, all ye that labour and are heavy laden, and I will give you rest. Take my yoke upon you, and learn of me; for I am meek and lowly in heart: and ye shall find rest unto your soul* **(Matthew 11:28-30)**.

"When You are Going Through Pain, The Lord Will Take Away The Cane"

And God shall wipe away all tears from their eyes; and there shall be no more death, neither sorrow, nor crying, neither shall there be any more pain: for the former things are passed away **(Revelation 21:4)**.

"Speak The Solution And Not The Situation"

Whoso keepeth his mouth and his tongue keepeth his soul from troubles **(Proverbs 21:23)**.

"The Enemy Is Loose, But He Is Running Out Of Juice"

And when the thousand years are expired, Satan shall be loosed out of his prison, And shall go out to deceive the nations which are in the four quarters of the earth, Gog and Magog, to gather them together to battle: the number of whom is as the sand of the sea. And they went up on the breadth of the earth, and compassed the camp of the saints about, and the beloved city: and fire came down from God out of heaven, and devoured them. And the devil that deceived them was cast into the lake of fire and brimstone, where the beast and the false prophet are, and shall be tormented day and night for ever and ever **(Revelations 20:7-10)**.

"A Sound Mind Is A Found Mind"

Seek ye the Lord while he may be found, call ye upon him while he is near **(Isaiah 55:6)**: *For God hath not given us the spirit of fear; but of power, and of love, and of a sound mind* **(2 Timothy 1:7)**.

"The Devil Will Try To Stop You, But The Lord Won't Drop You"

Fear none of those things which thou shalt suffer: behold, the devil shall cast some of you into prison, that ye may be tried; and ye shall have tribulation ten days: be thou faithful unto death, and I will give thee a crown of life **(Revelation 2:10)**.

"I'm Too Close To Call A Close"

For ye have need of patience, that, after ye have done the will of God, ye might receive the promise. For yet a little while, and he that shall come will come, and will not tarry. Now the just shall live by faith: but if any man draw back, my soul shall have no pleasure in him. But we are not of them who draw back unto perdition; but of them that believe to the saving of the soul **(Hebrews 10:36-39)**.

"The Food Of Life Is The Fruit Of Life"

Every branch in me that beareth not fruit he taken away: and every branch that beareth fruit, he purgeth it, that it may bring forth more fruit **(John 15:2)**.

312

"Take Dominion Over Opinion"

And straightway Jesus constrained his disciples to get into a ship, and to go before him unto the other side, while he sent the multitudes away. And when he had sent the multitudes away, he went up into a mountain apart to pray: and when the evening was come, he was there alone. But the ship was now in the midst of the sea, tossed with waves: for the wind was contrary. And in the fourth watch of the night Jesus went unto them, walking on the sea. And when the disciples saw him walking on the sea, they were troubled, saying, It is a spirit; and they cried out for fear. But straightway Jesus spake unto them, saying, Be of good cheer; it is I; be not afraid. And Peter answered him and said, Lord, if it be thou, bid me come unto thee on the water. And he said, Come. And when Peter was come down out of the ship, he walked on the water, to go to Jesus. But when he saw the wind boisterous, he was afraid; and beginning to sink, he cried, saying, Lord, save me. And immediately Jesus stretched forth [his] hand, and caught him, and said unto him, O thou of little faith, wherefore didst thou doubt? And when they were come into the ship, the wind ceased. Then they that were in the ship came and worshipped him, saying, Of a truth thou art the Son of God (Matthew 14:22-33). Behold, I give unto you power to tread on serpents and scorpions, and over all the power of the enemy: and nothing shall by any means hurt you (Luke 10:19).

"Getting On Fire For The Lord Through Prayer"

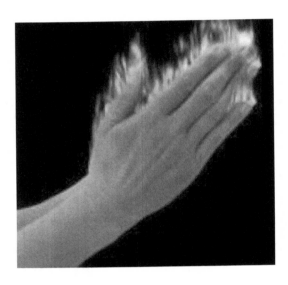

*Every man's work shall be made manifest: for the day shall be revealed by fire; and the fire shall try every man's work of what sort it is. If any man's work abide which he hath built thereupon, he shall receive a reward. If any man's work shall be burned, he shall suffer loss: but he himself shall be saved; yet so as by fire **(I Corithians 3:13-15)**. I indeed baptize you with water unto repentance: but he that cometh after me is mightier than I, whose shoes I am not worthy to bear: He shall baptize you with the Holy Ghost, and with fire **(Matthew 3:11)**: But we will give ourselves continually to prayer, and to the ministry of the word **(Acts 6:4)**.*

ABOUT THE AUTHOR

With the publication of Brandon T. Mitchell's second novel, He has many unique flowing thoughts that the Lord, God, births into his mind, day by day. As they become overwhelming, he wants to share his knowledge with others. Brandon T. Mitchell, at many times, was misunderstood, but his educational background proves him to be more advanced than what many individuals labeled him to be. He has a Bachelor's Degree from Tennessee State University in Family and Consumer Sciences with a Concentration in Interior Design, and a MBA in Accounting with a 4.0 GPA from Jones International University. Many down falls in the past has only made Brandon T. Mitchell a stronger person in life. He is a fighter for what he believes, and never gives up on his dreams.

41666929R00195

Made in the USA
Charleston, SC
04 May 2015